T I

A 21-Day Devotional to ⸏ ⸏ ⸏ ꞏꞏ ꞏ ꞏ ꞏ ꞏ ꞏᴜᴜꞏ Mind After Being Sidelined,

Disappointed or

Knocked Off Course

Karen Brown Tyson

Published by Constant Communicators, LLC.™

Copyright © 2021 by Karen Brown Tyson
Published by Constant Communicators, LLC.™

Most of the book's Scriptures are taken from The Holy Bible, English Standard Version. ESV® Text Edition: 2016. Copyright © 2001 by Crossway Bibles, a publishing ministry of Good News Publishers.

Additional Scripture is taken from:

Holy Bible: Easy-to-Read Version (ERV). International Edition © 2013, 2016 by Bible League International and used by permission.

Evans, Tony. *The Tony Evans Study Bible: Advancing God's Kingdom Agenda*. Nashville: Holman Bible Publishers, 2019. Print.

The Living Bible copyright © 1971 by Tyndale House Foundation. Used by permission of Tyndale House Publishers Inc., Carol Stream, Illinois 60188. All rights reserved.

The Message. Copyright © 1993, 1994, 1995, 1996, 2000, 2001, 2002. Used by permission of NavPress Publishing Group.

The Mission of God Study Bible © 2012 Holman Christian Standard Bible Copyright © 1999, 2000, 2002, 2003, 2009. Holman Bible Publishers. All rights reserved.

New American Standard Bible. Copyright © 1960, 1962, 1963, 1968, 1971, 1972, 1973, 1975, 1977, 1995 by The Lockman Foundation

New King James Version®. Copyright © 1982 by Thomas Nelson. Used by permission. All rights reserved.

The Voice™. Copyright © 2012 by Ecclesia Bible Society. Used by permission. All rights reserved.

Printed in the United States of America. All rights reserved under International Copyright Law. Contents and/or cover may not be reproduced in whole or in part in any form without the express written consent of the Publisher.

1

Heavenly Father,

When did you last appear right in front of my eyes, but I ignored you? Who did you send to me for a word of hope, and I neglected to open my mouth? When was the last time you called me, but I failed to answer? Forgive me, Lord.

Create in me a clean heart, and renew in me the right spirit.

Please open my eyes to see those in need. Touch my heart to respond to the cries of your people. Use my hands and feet to serve others whenever you call me.

Work through me to shine your light of grace. Help me to put your compassion and love on display for the world to see.

It's time to reset.

In The Name of Jesus,

Amen.

TABLE OF CONTENTS

God has a plan for my life. However, it took me a long time to see God's plans ahead of my plans. In both my personal and professional life, I'm used to making plans. After all, plans are what help us move through our day-to-day lives. We make plans to go to college, to move to a new city, or to retire. But as life unfolded in unexpected ways, I had to realize God's plans were part of his will for my life. In other words, it was always going to be God's way. How do we know? God's word reminds us, *People might make many plans, but what the Lord says is what will happen.* (Proverbs 19:21).

Do I still believe in making plans? Absolutely. But once I learned the importance of yielding to God's plan, I started writing all my plans in pencil. Ready to erase anything that doesn't fit with God's plan. So when life happens, and I feel sidelined, disappointed, or knocked off course, I remember God's promise to restore the people of Judah following their captivity,

I say this because I know the plans that I have for you." This message is from the Lord. "I have good plans for you. I don't plan to hurt you. I plan to give you hope and a good future. (Jeremiah 29:11).

This beloved scripture helps people find hope in knowing that God has a plan for everyone. But this declaration of hope requires action. God instructs Jeremiah to tell the people,

Then you will call my name. You will come to me and pray to me, and I will listen to you. You will search for me, and when you search for me with all your heart, you will find me. (Jeremiah 29:12-13).

But this promise of restoration will only come when God's people repent and seek him in a new way. I came to realize that part of knowing God's plan for my life involves effort on my part.

- First, I have to be willing to repent and seek God beyond mere church attendance.
- Next, no matter what challenges I face in life, I have an opportunity to become what God wants me to be.
- Finally, I can use my moments on the sidelines as a time to refresh my faith.

But for all of this to happen, I must reset my focus.

God wants us to focus on him, whether times are good or bad. He doesn't expect to come in second place in our life. But it can be hard to focus on God when your life gets turned upside down. Feelings of sadness, anger, or despair make us want to withdraw from people, and sometimes, God. The last thing the enemy wants us to do is read our Bibles, pray, or go to church. Those feelings of disappointment and rejection are what Satan uses to turn us away from God.

Time to Reset

Following a job layoff in 2017, I decided to use 2018 as my year to refresh. I was eager about the next chapter in my life. I asked God daily to reveal his plans for my life. By March, I started a new business called Constant Communicators. By August, I was the author of my first published book, *Time to Refresh: A 21-Day Devotional to Renew Your Mind After Being Laid Off, Fired, or Sidelined.* By October, I officially added the title, blogger, to my name with the launch of my new blog, Write to Inspire. I was amazed at what God allowed me to accomplish in 2018. But deep down inside, I knew God's plan for me involved more.

Before midnight on December 31, 2018, I heard a powerful sermon by Dr. T.L. Carmichael, Sr. titled, Reset Your Priorities. The sermon focused on Joel 2:25-26.

> *"I, the Lord, sent my army against you. The swarming locusts and the hopping locusts and the destroying locusts and the cutting locusts ate everything you had. But I will pay you back for those years of trouble.*

The central message in the Book of Joel is about "the day of the Lord." Throughout scripture, "the day of the Lord" is used in times when God sent judgment on his people. But the overall message relates to the future "day of the Lord," when Christ will return to set up his kingdom. In preparation for Christ's return, God's people must be ready.

There it was, straight from God. If I wanted to move on to more incredible things in 2019, I would need to reset some things in my life, like my faith, my finances, my mind. I was up for the challenge.

How to read this book

If you are someone whose life has been interrupted, or if you want to reset a few things in your life, this book is for you. Using the same approach I used in *Time to Refresh*, I focus on different topics each day and offer key takeaways around what I learned. The book will lead you on a 21-day journey of discovery and study where you will see how God moved in the lives of his people in the Bible.

Each day highlights:

— notes from my journal

— a topic I decided to focus on during my time of reset

— an example from the Bible that helped me see each topic in action

— my takeaways from each lesson

— advice on how to deal with real-life concerns

To help you apply the lessons to your life, I offer my GLOW philosophy, which stands for:

Grateful. Each day, we will end our lesson by letting God know how grateful we are for all he is doing during our reset period.

Listening. We will listen to God as we meditate and pray.

Observation. We will pay careful attention to what God wants to show us in his word.

Witness. We will witness to others as we share our 'timeout' testimonies.

Open your heart to what God wants you to get out of this study. Ask the Lord to give you new revelations each day.

My prayer is that you will gain a deeper understanding of God's plan for your life. I hope that you will come away understanding that when God allows us to be sidelined, disappointed, or knocked off course, there's an opportunity to go through a transformation that will not only bless us but will deepen our walk with Christ.

Peace and blessings,

Karen

Note to self:

Dear Lord,

I am so blessed to wake up this morning to see a brand new day. This is the day that the Lord has made, and I plan to rejoice. I understand life is about calibration and change. My prayer, Lord, is that you change me from the inside out. I'm ready for a new year and a new me. I can't wait to see where you lead me and what you have planned for my life. I'm ready for a change.

Lead me on.

DAY 1 - TIME TO CHANGE MY OUTFIT

Trust the Lord completely, and don't depend on your knowledge. With every step you take, think about what he wants, and he will help you go the right way.

Proverbs 3:5-6

My mother let me enroll in an after-school sewing class when I was in high school. I enjoyed it. The way the thread passed through the sewing machine to weave pieces of fabric into clothing was so amazing. My aunt, Jess, was one of the best parts of my sewing career. She was also a tailor, attending classes at a local tailor's shop at night. She would take me to JoAnn Fabrics to get everything I needed for my sewing projects. I loved looking through the Vogue pattern catalogs for outfits and then going through the large file cabinet-type drawers to pull out patterns.

Learning how to sew opened my eyes to so many things. Before long, I learned how to alter the patterns slightly to work in my design ideas. By the time I left the class, I knew how to make the kind of clothes I wanted to wear. I learned how to make something out of nothing. The course taught me a lot about sewing and myself. But the experience also taught me about God.

Just like a fashion designer makes elegant clothes, God has unique plans for my beautiful life. He cuts every pattern to suit me perfectly. God chooses only the finest material, understanding when silk will work better than cotton. To ensure my life fits me exactly, he cuts patterns just for me. Once he has the garment assembled, God doesn't mind making alterations if necessary. Like a tailor, he cuts out parts of my life that no longer fit. God is the ultimate designer.

So when I got laid off in 2017, I knew I was getting a new outfit. From the moment I learned the company would eliminate my job, I decided to trust God. Using Proverbs 3 as my guide, I focused on what it means to trust God in every situation. I knew how important it would be for me to trust God wholeheartedly and that I didn't have to figure everything out on my own (verse 5). I listened to everything God told me to do and go everywhere he told me to go (verse 6). The new design God created for my life was going to be one of his finest creations yet.

In allowing Proverbs 3 to act as a blueprint, I didn't spend countless hours worrying about what God was doing. I didn't try to figure out why the company laid me off. There were no sleepless nights. No soul-searching. No tears or fears. I knew immediately that God was making alterations and that the job I had been doing for the past 16 years no longer fit my life. I was excited to change into a new outfit.

Timeout Takeaways

Learn to see the threads that connect my life.

In preparation for my last day of work, I had to tell myself that everything I was going through was part of a bigger plan orchestrated by God. I didn't want to be a person who talked about faith but never walked by faith. As far as I was concerned, my glass was half full, not half empty. Instead of imagining my life as tattered rags unraveling, I chose to see the beauty in the threads that connect my life experiences.

A good fitting is key to a great outfit.

One of the most critical parts of the garment-making process is fitting. A tailor must measure the client to make a pattern for the garment. Often tailors use muslin, an inexpensive fabric used for making test garments before they begin sewing with the actual fabric selected for the garment. At every phase, the tailor works to ensure the garment fits the client during each fitting. If the fit of the garment is off, the tailor makes changes as needed. The client, eager to get the finished product, waits with excitement for the new outfit. I saw the next job God was preparing for me in the same way. I knew my next assignment would be the perfect fit. I just had to be willing to wait. During the waiting period, I had a chance to wear a garment of praise instead of a disheartened spirit (Isaiah 61:3).

One size does not fit all.

At the start of my career, I looked at the career paths of other public relations professionals. I mapped out a plan that included projected job titles by specific dates in my career path. Years ago, I thought I would have a vice president title by the time I turned 50. But once I turned my attention to Christ and his mission, that plan went out the window. My original plan relied on my knowledge, skills, and ability to make it as far as possible in my career. But when I decided to trust God to design my life and career, I found out that one size does not fit all. Little did I know that God wanted me to become the CEO of my own company.

GRATEFUL

What are you grateful for today?

LISTENING

Ask God to provide clear instructions on anything you need to change about yourself.

OBSERVATION

Read Proverbs 3.

WITNESS

Talk to someone about how you trust God during times of change.

DAY 2 - TIME TO ASK FOR DIRECTIONS

Note to self:

Good morning, Holy Spirit.

I am waking up this morning a blessed woman. I am grateful for my family, health, and your provision for my life.

As I walk into the newness of life, I don't want to wander around aimlessly. Thank you for your New Year's Eve message about resetting my priorities. Show me where I can do better. I am ready for you to order my steps.

I am ready.

Change Your Life

But there's also this, it's not too late—

God's personal Message!—

"Come back to me and really mean it!

Come fasting and weeping, sorry for your sins!"

Joel 2:12

The first job I got right out of college carried me to the beautiful state of North Carolina. A big part of my job as a public relations account executive involved me driving from city to city for client meetings. I would print out directions for every road trip (there were no Smartphones or driving apps back then). One day after work, I decided to take my brother, who was visiting, shopping at an outlet mall. On the way to the mall, I followed the directions a friend had given me. On the way home, I decided to go a different route using my memory and the highway signs. Big mistake. What should have been a 45-minute drive turned into a 90-minute drive.

I discovered the same thing happens when I don't follow God's direction. Every time I try to go my own way or when I stray away from God's guidance, I get lost. I start going down unnecessary paths. I end up in unlikely places. And the only way I can get back on track is to run back to God's instruction - either through his Holy word or through his Holy Spirit.

The people in Joel 2 had the same problem. In verse two, God sends a personal message to his people. God sends Joel to tell the people to return to him. Despite all they had done, God was ready to welcome them back. But God didn't want the people to return any kind of way. He needed repentance from them. God said, "Come back to me, come back and really mean it! Come fasting and crying, sorry for your sins." (v.12) God asks his children in the Bible to return to him when they get lost. But God needs repentance upon our return. He wants us to be doers of the word, not merely hearers. (James 1:22).

God ordered me to take a timeout from working at the beginning of 2018. At first, I saw my job layoff as an opportunity to rest, relax, and refresh. But I believe Christ wanted me to evaluate my relationship with Him. What bad habits had I adopted that now needed to go away? How many times in the past year had I gone my own way instead of following God's directions? What things do I need to change in my life to prepare for the coming of Christ? It was time for me to take a long hard look in the mirror about the obstacles, including the sin, I allowed to creep into my life.

Timeout Takeaways

Be open to change.

We often say it's hard to accept change, but that isn't entirely true. Just think about the change that comes when we have a baby or when we adopt a child. Although we might be slightly nervous, we quickly swing into action to welcome our newest family member. Most times, the change we resist has to do with things we don't want to give up. But sometimes, the change we resist is precisely the change needed to improve our life. In Joel 2:12, God encourages people to change their lives, not just their clothes. Despite their sins and mistakes, God invited the people to come back to him. The reason is that God is also Elohim Chasidic, God of lovingkindness. God is forgiveness, gracious and compassionate, slow to anger, and abounding in lovingkindness (Nehemiah 9:17).

Live a lifestyle of repentance.

The enemy presents us with a myriad of opportunities to sin. But if we confess our sins, he is faithful and righteous to forgive us our sins and cleanse us from all unrighteousness (1 John 1:9). God calls every believer to live a righteous life. But

17

living right requires thought, preparation, and repentance. We can't just say, "I know I'm wrong, but God knows my heart," every time we decide to curse at the driver in front of us. True repentance requires action. We must change by not choosing sin. Do followers of God make mistakes? Absolutely. But the key is not to continue making the same sinful mistakes over and over again. Seeking forgiveness is critical.

Ask God for direction.

God wants to help his creation. The only problem is sometimes we like to go off on our own without direction. In the example where I went to the mall with my brother, I followed MapQuest's directions. Even though I had never been to that mall before, I followed the directions before I started driving. But on the way home, I decided to take a different route with no idea where I was going. God wants to help us find our way. But to do so, we must connect with him daily through prayer and his word.

GRATEFUL

What are you grateful for today?

LISTENING

Ask God to show you the areas of your life where you are falling short.

OBSERVATION

Read Joel 2.

WITNESS

Pick one person you trust and tell them one thing you plan to change this month.

DAY 3 - TIME TO REMEMBER MY FIRST LOVE

Note to self:

Good morning, Lord.

Thank you for reminding me of your love and grace. As I start each day not knowing what lies ahead, help me remember that you will make my path straight as long as I trust you. I can remember a time when I was lost and unfocused. As I walk into the newness of the day, I don't want to wander around aimlessly. Please show me where I can do better. I am ready for you to order my steps.

Thank you for being the God of second chances.

"But I have this against you: You have left the love you had in the beginning. So remember where you were before you fell. Change your hearts and do what you did at first. If you don't change, I will come to you and remove your lampstand from its place."

(Revelation 2:4-5)

I asked my mother if I could join the school band when I was in fifth grade. Without looking up from folding the laundry, she asked, "How much is it?" to which I replied, 'Ten dollars for the school year.' She said she would think about it. My mother was careful to handle our expenses because my father had died one month before I asked to join the band. And since we did not have a lot of money, ten dollars was a big deal.

As I headed out the door the next day to school, I saw the ten dollars on the table. I was so excited. I practically ran to school. I knew which instrument I wanted to play. When I got to music class, I proudly turned in my ten dollars, and my teacher allowed me to go into the storage room to pick out my instrument. My eyes darted around the cramped little storage room, looking for the instrument I knew I was born to play. After looking past what seemed like hundreds of clarinets, a few tubas, and the trumpets, I finally found the instrument of my dreams: the flute.

In the weeks and months to come, I would practice my flute for hours. After a few weeks, our music teacher took us all over town to perform. One day, we performed downtown in the city center. People who worked in offices and department stores came out to listen to our performance. My mother was in the crowd too. I could hardly contain myself. I just wanted her to be proud of her ten-dollar investment.

With great passion, I played the flute for two years. But something had changed by the time I went to junior high school. It seemed that playing the flute would no longer fit my life. I lost my love for the flute.

The church of Ephesus lost its passion for Christ. At first glance, the church's work was impressive. In Jesus's letter to Ephesus, he commended them for being hardworking and for never giving up (v. 2). The church did not accept evil people and tested those who claimed to be apostles (v. 2). The church of Ephesus refused to throw in the towel when things got rough.

But where the church fell short is revealed in verse 4, when Jesus says, "But you walked away from your first love - why? What's going on with you, anyway?" What did Jesus mean by "first love"? The passionate pursuit of Christ. While it was true the church of Ephesus was busy getting on with what Christ asked them to do, somewhere along the way, they lost their passion. What started as a zeal for Christ turned into ritualistic service. Jesus could see how the church of Ephesus was going through the motions.

But Jesus's letter to the church of Ephesus is a preventative message to every church and believer. Jesus urged the Ephesians to, "Turn back! Recover your dear early love." (v. 5) Christ is not interested in being second, third, or last in any believer's life. If any Christian takes a spiritual detour that diverts attention away from Christ, there must be repentance. Jesus said, "No time to waste, for I'm well on my way to removing your light from the golden circle." (v. 5) Without repentance, Christ would put out the church's light.

From the moment we surrender our lives to Christ, the enemy tries to throw obstacles in our way to distract us. But as followers of Christ, we must stay vigilant in protecting our passion for Christ. Spiritual dullness will set in if we are not careful. In the end, the love we had for Christ when we let Him into our lives for the first time will soon vanish. In our hearts, we must hold Jesus first.

Timeout Takeaways

Don't forget to put first things first.

Eleven years before I started my career as a public relations account executive, I gave my life to Christ. In the beginning, I was so excited to serve the Lord. After I graduated from college and added the responsibility of a full-time job to my schedule, I pushed God to the back-burner. Sometimes I just went through the motions, and other times I was motionless. I focused on my new career and getting ahead to the next job. As a result, I would move from one task to the next and not think twice about praying, reading my Bible, or sharing the gospel. I lost the love I felt for Christ when I first surrendered my life to Him. But one day, I decided to repent and turn my attention to God's kingdom and what he wants me to do. (Matt 6:33) Once I put God first, I stood on his word, and he gave me everything I needed.

Don't forget the pursuit.

To have a meaningful relationship with Christ must involve pursuit. What does this look like for present-day Christians? It means showing up for service to God's people early and eager. It means being intentional about sharing your testimony with others. It means creating a personal discipleship plan to ensure growth in God's kingdom. For me, it means being ready and willing to use my spiritual gifts from the moment God calls my name. While I believe I can do all things through Christ who strengthens me, I don't think I must do everything. Therefore, I look for opportunities to build other disciples and guide them in using their spiritual gifts according to God's plan and the local church's needs.

Don't forget faithfulness.

God has many names. One of his names, El Emunah, means faithful God. In Deuteronomy 7:9:

> Know therefore that the Lord your God is God; he is the faithful God [El Emunah], keeping his covenant of love to a thousand generations of those who love him and keep his commandments.

The steadfast love of God motivates me to strive for faithfulness. Will I ever be able to match God's faithfulness? Never. But in remembering my first love for Christ and his love for me, I press toward the mark. (Philippians 3:14)

GRATEFUL

What are you grateful for today?

LISTENING

Ask God to help you see any areas you can improve in your relationship with him.

OBSERVATION

Read Revelation 2.

WITNESS

Share your testimony about how you gave your life to Christ.

DAY 4 - TIME TO COME CLOSER

Note to self:

Good Morning, Lord!

Your word reminds me to seek you while you may be found. So here I am to praise your name. I know that anyone can come to you in prayer, and you will listen. Please forgive me and wipe away my sins. As I open my heart to your plans for my life, let me see life through your eyes. Please take away all doubt and fear. I shake off every obstacle trying to keep me from getting closer to you. Thank you for your blessings.

Let your light shine through me as I go out into the world.

DAY 4 - TIME TO COME CLOSER

There, the angel of the Lord appeared to him in flames of fire from within a bush. Moses saw that though the bush was on fire, it did not burn up. So Moses thought, "I will go over and see this strange sight—why the bush does not burn up."

Exodus 3:2-3

For years I wore contact lenses in both eyes to improve my vision. In my right eye, I am farsighted and nearsighted in the left eye. Contact lenses help me to see correctly out of both eyes. But one year, during a routine eye exam, the doctor made a remarkable discovery. Without any contact lenses in my eyes, the doctor asked me to read a series of eye charts. Some of the letters on the charts seemed close, while other letters seemed far away. She would ask each time, "Which line is clearer on the chart?" After examining five eye charts, the doctor advised me that I just needed a contact lens in my right eye. She explained how my left eye improved since my last eye exam. My vision changed.

Sometimes God wants to change our vision so we will see things his way. In Exodus 3, we find Moses sitting on the sideline of life. After murdering at age 40, Moses runs away to the land of Midian. During his period of exile, 40 years passed, during which time Moses married Zipporah and built a life. While tending to the sheep, an angel of the Lord appears to Moses in the fire in a bush. Moses cannot believe his eyes and decides to get a closer look at the burning bush. Little did Moses know that God used the burning bush to change his vision.

As Moses moved closer to the bush, God stopped Moses to prepare him for being in the presence of the Lord. "Take off your sandals, for the place where you are standing is holy ground." (v. 5). After God got Moses' attention and told him how to prepare for their conversation, God made it clear that he was the true God. Knowing what it meant to be in the presence of God, Moses covered his face and listened to God's invitation to come out of hiding. "It's time for you to go back: I'm sending you to Pharoah." (v. 10) God wanted Moses to go back to Egypt to rescue the Israelites.

God always invites us to get close to him. The invitation's significance isn't based on our accomplishments, race, wealth, job title, or gender. No. God wants us to come closer to him simply because he loves us. God wants us to spend time with him. Talk to him. Listen to him to find out about our next assignment. Like Moses, I have been on the sidelines more than a few times in my life. My most recent time was when I decided to take God up on his offer to come closer. During that time, I learned so much about God and about what he has planned for me.

Timeout Takeaways

Change your perspective.

By the time I started my first job as an assistant account executive at a PR agency, I had figured out my whole career. I planned every step I would take for the next 20 years. But in reality, things didn't happen the way I planned. While I still love a good plan, I learned how to change my perspective and go with God's plan for my life. Once I decided to let go and let God, everything fell into place.

Change your position.

God invited Moses to come off the sidelines of life to bring Israel's people out of Egypt. To operate within God's plan, Moses had to move. Moses' story reminds me that today may not be where God wants me to be tomorrow. As I ask God to bless me with new opportunities, I realize that I might need to change my position — take a new job, work in a different industry, or travel to another state to talk to people who want to learn something new. I might have to move.

Change your priorities.

When I was in my 20s, I thought I would be a vice president by the time I reached my 50s. But my priorities changed. In the years leading up to 2017, I focused less on how I could climb the corporate ladder and more on how I could help others grow in grace. By the time I reached my 50s, I didn't care about getting to the top of my career mountain as much as I cared about helping people solve problems or follow their dreams. Being laid off helped me to see God's vision for my life. Once my priorities changed, God showed me that my dream of becoming a vice president in someone else's company was never part of his plan. Instead, God led me to become the president of my own business.

GRATEFUL

What are you grateful for today?

LISTENING

Ask God to provide clear directions on where he wants you to go.

OBSERVATION

Read Exodus 3.

WITNESS

Tell one person about a time when you were headed in one direction, and God stepped in to order your steps in a different direction.

DAY 5 — TIME TO COME OUT OF THE DARK

Note to self:

Heavenly Father, when I see your favor over my life, I am so grateful.

Thank you for fighting for me. Forgive me when I couldn't see clearly, and I worried about things you had under control. Lord, I let go of all doubt, fear and worry. I stand today on the promises of your word. Thank you for being so loving and faithful.

Ready to move forward into the blessings of today.

But I trust in Your faithful love; my heart leaps at the thought of imminent deliverance by You.

Psalm 13:5

In 2012, Logan Eliasen explored a cave in the Maquoketa Caves State Park when he got stuck. Logan, a 20-year-old theology student, tried to free himself, but the more he tried, the harder it was to move. Over 20 hours, rescuers from two states tried to free Logan from the cave. To get through the ordeal, Logan prayed. Logan believes prayer is the only thing that kept him going throughout the entire ordeal.

We all have cave-like experiences at some point, where we feel stuck, isolated, or abandoned. In Psalm 13, we hear David calling out to God in a hopeless situation. Although it is not clear where David is or why he cries out to God, we know that he feels betrayed by God. David asks God, "How long will you forget about me and look the other way." (v. 1) Feeling alone, David wants to know how long he will feel the sadness in his heart (v. 2). David tells God about the agony he feels because he doesn't believe God is near. He begs God to turn around and respond to his cries (v. 3). During his time of suffering, David reflects on how happy his enemies will be to see him fail (v. 4).

I know exactly how David felt. My first year in undergraduate school did not go as planned. In addition to going to school full time at night, I worked a full-time job during the day. Attending college was a lot harder than I thought it would be, and eventually, I flunked out. Not once but twice. I was devastated because I knew my journey included a college education. I remember crying out to God, begging him to let me go to a new school. My decision to not tell my family initially only added to my pain. Carrying around such a heavy secret left me feeling defeated and alone. But God was with me the entire time. My situation turned around when God sent a small group of extraordinary people to help me get into a new school.

It's common to hear present-day followers of Christ say, "But, God." The word *but* means on the contrary or the other hand. Used as a conjunction in a sentence, the word but connects and creates a transition between two clauses. Between verses 1 and 4, David tells God why he needs to be heard. In verse 5, David transitions from a desperate cry to praise. David tells the Lord, but I will trust in your faithful love (v. 5). Upon remembering God's goodness and faithfulness, David has a "but, God" moment. Just the thought of being freed by God not only causes David's heart to leap but causes David to sing. (v. 5-6).

God wants us to recall the moments in our lives when he saved us from dark places. Like Logan, the young man stuck in a cave; God needs us to know that when we call upon him, he hears us. To get us out of every tight spot, God needs us to believe him. Like David, I had a lot of "but, God" moments. Once I gave up the guilt and shame of flunking out of the college and allowed God to step in, I was accepted at a new university. But before I got there, I started trusting and praising God. Just like that, God rescued me from the darkness.

Timeout Takeaways

Pray your way out.

When God allows challenges to come into our lives where we feel trapped and alone, he is waiting for us to call him in prayer. He's not waiting for our husbands, or mothers, or friends to call him on our behalf (although he will receive their prayers for us). Yet, prayer is sometimes the last thing we do. Convinced I could handle everything on my own, I spent days and weeks trying to get into another school. But when I finally got on my knees and prayed, God turned everything around. God is waiting to hear from us individually. Our faith in God has to be personal.

Praise your way out.

Convinced that God would rescue him, David promised the Lord he would sing to him. Years ago, whenever I went through cave-like experiences, I found it hard to praise the Lord. I focused more on the problem and less on God's ability to take care of the problem. But with each challenge, I learned to praise the Lord. Once I learned to praise God through every situation, everything changed. God's Holy Spirit brought me peace, focus, and clear direction in dealing with difficult situations where I felt alone. God deserves praise and worship, whether times in our lives are good or bad.

Petition your way out.

At the 20th hour, the volunteers trying to rescue Logan changed shifts. During this time, Logan was left alone. Determined not to give up, Logan cried out to God one last time, saying, "God, I don't have anything left. If there was any chance that I could free myself, it's gone. I need you now." With what little strength he had, Logan braced his hands to the rock and started to move. God never left Logan alone in that cave. God doesn't leave us alone, either. We must be willing to call out to God no matter how tired or weary we get.

GRATEFUL

What are you grateful for today?

LISTENING

Ask God to help you deal with any challenge in your life, causing you to feel alone, trapped, or abandoned.

OBSERVATION

Read Psalm 13.

WITNESS

Share your cave experience story with one person and tell them how God brought you out.

DAY 6 — TIME TO PUT THE PAST IN THE PAST

Note to self:

Dear God,

I believe today will be a great day because this is the day you made. I am going to rejoice today. I'm not going to worry about what I was doing this time last year. There have been times when I wouldn't let go of the past. But not today.

I look forward to the future and everything you have planned for me. Your plan for my life is better than anything I could ever imagine. You have already blessed me above all I could ask or think.

I am walking in victory.

"Forget about what's happened; don't keep going over old history. Be alert; be present. I'm about to do something brand-new. It's bursting out! Don't you see it? There it is! I'm making a road through the desert, rivers in the badlands.

Isaiah 43:18-19

Mark Twain once said, "You can't depend on your eyes when your imagination is out of focus." With this in mind, how we see circumstances in life can influence our destiny.

The disappointment that comes with the end of a relationship or the loss of a job is natural. Breakups are hard. If we're not careful, we can let the feeling of rejection spiral out of control. Days and weeks of emotional torment can leave us rehashing the past and asking questions like: 'Why me? Why now?'

Like so many people, I got laid off in November 2017. After deciding to make a business strategy shift, the company I worked for was letting me go by the end of the year. Just like that, my job came to an abrupt end. In the moments after hearing the news, I made one of the most important decisions of my life. I turned to God. At that moment, I believed that if God allowed my job to end,

35

then he had something better planned for me. So, what did I do? I decided to let them go. At the same hour, I learned the company was letting me go; I decided to let my employer go, too. Not from a place of bitterness or anger. But from a place of peace.

In the book of Isaiah, God makes a promise of restoration to the people of Israel in chapters 40 to 48. After 70 years of Babylonian captivity, it was time for Israel's restoration to Zion (40:1-11). To prepare for the journey, Isaiah appealed to the people by reminding them of the departure their ancestors made out of Egypt (v. 16). The prophet recounts the powerful story of how God's people, once trapped in slavery in Egypt, were brought out of bondage and oppression. He tells them of a mighty God who stopped chariots and horses by drowning them in the sea. Isaiah assures the people that the same God who delivered their ancestors would do the same for them. While Isaiah felt the need to remind the people of God's miraculous acts from the past, he did not want them to limit God.

But Isaiah also tells the people not to spend too much time recounting past victories (43:18). Instead, he encouraged them to watch God closely because he had the power to perform even greater miracles than ever seen before. God said he would do something new (v. 19). His promise to make a road in the desert and rivers that flowed through dry land should have motivated the people. Through faith and imagination, God wanted the people to know that he had great plans for them.

Timeout Takeaways

Don't forget what God has done.

If God brings you out of one tight spot, he can get you out of another. The Israelites often forgot what God did for them. In Deuteronomy 8, Moses reminded the Israelites of how God provided for them throughout their 40-year journey through the wilderness. During that time, the Israelites saw God's faithfulness on full display as he provided food, clothing, water, and protection. Whenever I find myself forgetting, I think about how God brought me out of every job layoff and every difficult situation in my life.

Don't hold on to the past.

In my final days at work, people were kind and wished me well. And I felt the same way about them and the company. I was happy to finish all of my projects and pass on information I hoped would help my co-workers continue to do the work I was leaving behind. From the time I gave God total control, I had no hard feelings. For me, letting go was not about being vengeful or bitter. Instead, letting go was about not holding on to the past. I didn't spend one-minute wishing I still worked at a company that no longer wanted me. In the days following my departure from the company, I didn't see the need to catch up on the latest company news to stay in the know. As I checked my social media accounts, I didn't feel obligated to retweet, share, or like anything my former employer posted on social media. I was determined to let go of the past. (Isaiah 43:18) But I couldn't do it without God's help. God's Holy Spirit led me on a path of peace.

Don't fear the journey ahead.

Exodus 14 highlights the Israelites' exodus out of Egypt. When the Israelites saw Pharaoh and his army coming toward them, they were terrified but cried to the Lord for help (v. 10). But Moses told them not to be afraid of the road ahead. Instead, he encouraged them by saying, "Don't be scared! Don't run away! Stand where you are and watch the Lord save you today (v. 13). God tells Moses to raise his stick over the sea to part it so the Israelites could escape (v. 16). God wanted to show the Israelites that he was more powerful than Pharaoh. The same holds today for anyone trying to escape bondage. We must trust God. No matter where life takes us, we don't need to worry or be afraid. Just as Moses encouraged the Israelites not to fear the journey ahead, we too can be courageous because God promises to always be with us.

GRATEFUL

What are you grateful for today?

LISTENING

Ask God to provide clear instructions on anything you need to leave behind that has been holding you back from moving forward.

OBSERVATION

Read Isaiah 43.

WITNESS

Talk to someone about how you trust God during times of change.

DAY 7 — TIME TO CAST YOUR CARES

Note to self:

Lord, I thank you for the peace that comes with trusting you. I had to learn to embrace Proverbs 3 as I put my trust in you. No longer do I lean to my understanding. Please forgive me for the times I thought I knew better than you. Once I started to trust you fully, my sleep even improved. Please help me to become better in every area of my life.

I am so grateful you didn't give up on me, Lord.

So bow down under God's strong hand; then, when the time comes, God will lift you. Since God cares for you, let Him carry all your burdens and worries. Most importantly, be disciplined and stay on guard. Your enemy, the devil, is prowling around outside like a roaring lion, just waiting and hoping for the chance to devour someone.

1 Peter 5:6-8

One of the biggest struggles in my faith walk centered around one thing: control. Specifically, my inability to allow God to have total control over my life. Oh, sure, I would give God control over a few things in my life, like my move from Ohio to North Carolina to start my first job. But for years, I muddled along, thinking I could take care of most of my business myself. I was convinced that all I had to do was get everything all lined up like a row of dominos and allow God to knock them over for me. I had the perfect plan for everything. So I thought.

I was tired of bearing so many burdens inside me by the time I hit my 30s. It would be an understatement to say that the worries of this life weighed me down. When I think about wasting time and resources, trying to control all my concerns, I shake my head. Who did I think I was telling God to step aside while I figured out everything? Did I think that I knew better than the Lord Almighty? After years of frustration and disappointment, I finally learned that if my plans don't align with God's plans, I was wasting time. I was weary and wounded.

To begin the healing process, I turned to 1 Peter 5:6-8. After so many years of self-rule, I finally gave everything to God. But first, I had to humble myself and bow down under God's mighty hand (v. 6). In doing so, God showed me on more than one occasion that he would lift me when the time was right. Next, I let God take over all of my worries, burdens, and cares (v. 7). When my daycare plans fell through, I prayed. When I needed a new car, I went to God in prayer. When I found a lump on my back, I asked God to take care of the surgery. By the time I got laid off for the third time in my career, I gladly let Jesus take the wheel. Over the years, God has shown me the beauty in casting all my cares on him.

Although Satan may not be the cause of every issue in my life, he will not give up an opportunity to use it to his advantage. I had to learn, sometimes the hard way, that I have to trust in the Lord with all my heart and not lean on my understanding as he prowls around looking for ways to strike (Proverbs 3:5). Christ wants me, instead, to accept the peace he gives to all believers.

Allowing God to control every aspect of my life does not mean I live a dull and boring life. Nor does it mean I aimlessly walk around with no direction or focus. I still have dreams and goals. I always explore new ideas for the future. But instead of forging ahead on my own, I go to God in prayer first. I check in to see if my thoughts are part of God's plan. God has made us what we are. I know now that in Christ Jesus, I am a new person meant to spend my life doing the right things he has already planned for me to do. (Ephesians 2:10) I am grateful for a renewed mind.

Timeout Takeaways

Dump your burdens.

When I was weighed down with burdens, Satan often attacked me through my feelings. So many times, I let my emotions take over and cloud the truth of God's word. God does not want his children burdened down by the cares of this life. God asks us to lay our burdens down so he can take care of them. "Cast your burden on the Lord, and He shall sustain you; He shall never permit the righteous to be moved" (Psalm 55:22)

Grow in grace.

Our obsession with this world's cares can destroy the seeds God wants to plant in our lives. Luke 8:14 warns us about the seed that fell among the thorny weeds. The word tells us that it is like the people who hear God's teaching, but they let the worries, riches, and pleasures of this life stop them from growing.

So they never produce a crop. Can you imagine going through life never creating anything meaningful? Yet, this is the path some believers take when they become more consumed by the worries of life. I don't know about you but I want to produce a good crop. (v. 15)

Embrace peace.

We cannot live a peaceful life worrying. Satan knows that if he can get us to worry about our problems, we will be distracted from God and his instructions. But in John 16:33, Jesus tells us, "In this world, you will have troubles. But be brave! I have defeated the world!" Once I learned to embrace the peace Jesus talks about, my life changed. When trouble comes, as Jesus warned us it would, I know peace is available for me.

GRATEFUL

What are you grateful for today?

LISTENING

Ask God to provide clear instructions on anything you need to release to him.

OBSERVATION

Read 1 Peter 5.

WITNESS

Talk to someone about a time when you allowed God to lead you through a problem in your life.

WORDS OF ADVICE

I don't know how I'm supposed to get over the feeling of rejection that comes with being dismissed or asked to "sit this one out." People are used to seeing me out front, and I like the attention I get as the leader.

As the kid who was usually picked last for the school softball game, it felt good when I got selected to lead the marketing communications team. It was a role I felt qualified to fill. Soon, my work was recognized. It felt great to be out front leading a winning team. But as I moved to other positions in other companies, I had to learn to embrace the sidelines for several reasons.

I recognize that some people place great importance on being out front or being on top. In some instances, there is a belief that if you get selected as the leader, then you must be the best, the greatest, or the smartest. However, when you don't get picked, Satan will try to use your feelings of disappointment to his advantage. Before you know it, your feelings turn into anger, resentment, or jealousy. The enemy will even try to convince you that there is something wrong with you. You're not good enough or smart enough, or aggressive enough for the job. Forget those lies.

I learned to shut out all the noise around me and the negative self-talk to hear God's voice by going to God's word. I love Romans 8:31-32, where Paul reminds us of God's love for us through Jesus Christ.

> *So, what do you think? With God on our side like this, how can we lose? If God didn't hesitate to put everything on the line for us, embracing our condition and exposing himself to the worst by sending his own Son, is there anything else he wouldn't gladly and freely do for us?*

I find comfort in knowing that God is for me, no matter what happens in the world. To keep my ego in check, I turn to 1 Peter 5:6:

> *So be content with who you are, and don't put on airs. God's strong hand is on you; he'll promote you at the right time.*

Rather than worrying about what others think, I can rest knowing that when the time is right, God knows the right time for my next promotion and when I should receive praise. Without worrying about what it looks like to sit on the sidelines, I can embrace what God sees in me.

Do you find yourself feeling rejected while sitting on the sidelines? Here are a few things you can do:

Understand why you feel the need to be the leader. Use prayer and journal writing to explore how you feel about always being the leader. What's the best thing about being a leader? What's the worst thing about being asked to "sit this one out?" Be honest about how you feel.

Believe what God says about you. Go to God's word to find scriptures about God's love, grace, and provision for you. Record the scriptures that speak to your heart. Take time to reflect on your favorite passages of scripture.

Identify the benefits of sitting on the sidelines. What are some of the benefits of not being chosen as a leader? List some things you can do to help the person chosen to lead the team or project.

Ask God to help you with humility. To stay aligned with God's plans for our life, we must be humble and walk in humility.

Note to self:

Good morning, Heavenly Father,

Thanks for letting me see the start of a brand new day. Lead me to places you want me to go. Let me stay focused on your guiding light. I confess there have been times when I found it hard to focus on you and the things you called me to do. Please forgive me for not always being open and available when you called. I know you are searching for people to respond when you call. When you call me, Lord, I will answer.

Thank you for your amazing grace.

"Look at me. I stand at the door. I knock. If you hear me call and open the door, I'll come right in and sit down to supper with you. Conquerors will sit alongside me at the head table, just as I, having conquered, took the place of honor at the side of my Father. That's my gift to the conquerors!

Revelation 3:20-21

Two months after graduating from West Virginia University, I moved to North Carolina. Not wanting my mother to feel like I was too far from home, I called her every week. One weekend, I decided to go home to see my mother. I wanted to surprise her, so I didn't tell her I was coming. I called her for our weekly chat. Little did she know, I was standing outside her front door. When she heard the knock at the door, I could hear her say, "Who is it?" Not wanting to give away the surprise, I stayed silent. When she pulled back the curtain and saw it was me, Mommy was pleasantly surprised.

In Revelation 3:14-22, we find Jesus addressing the church of Laodicea. Before he begins his message, Jesus is already familiar with this church. He said, "you are neither cold nor hot." (v. 15) The church members are under the false impression that they don't need Christ because they have money. But they are only fooling themselves as Jesus points out they are wretched, pitiful, poor, blind, and naked (v. 17). The love of Christ comes with rebuke and discipline (v. 19).

At first glance, it may seem funny that Christ would knock on the door of a church. But a closer examination reveals that Jesus is not one to force himself on anyone. All that the Father gives me will come to me, and whoever comes to me I will never cast out. (John 6:37) Jesus is knocking on the door of the hearts of the people who are already in the church. His followers. Have you ever felt like Jesus was knocking on the door to your heart? I have. In my year of reset, I could hear the knock loud and clear.

God's word is full of invitations. Come to me (Matthew 11:28). Revelation 22:17 reminds us:

"The Spirit and the bride say, "Come!" Everyone who hears this should also say, "Come!" All who are thirsty may come; they can have the water of life as a gift if they want it."

Through God's word, we find invitations to enter into a deeper relationship with our Heavenly Father. All we have to do is let Jesus in.

Jesus goes on to say in verse 20, "If you hear me call and open the door, I will come right in and sit down with you for supper." By opening the door, we submit to God's will. In other words, we can have an intimate relationship with Jesus when we take him up on his offer. This invitation from Christ comes with an offer to have an elevated personal experience with Jesus (v. 21)

The Laodicean church opened my eyes to a dark reality about followers of Christ. Some in the church will not move from their spiritual laziness to let Jesus in. Despite being members of the church, some will not invite Christ into their lives. Yes, some church members attend church regularly. Perhaps they even volunteer. But they have not allowed Christ to come into their hearts completely. As the members of the Laodicean church, some present-day Christians keep Jesus on the outside looking in.

One of the hardest things for a Christian to do is surrender entirely to Christ. Instead, it seems more advantageous to chase the world. Looking at the Church of Laodicea caused me to examine my relationship with Christ. Was I guilty of leaving Christ out of my life? Did I suffer from spiritual slackness by not praying, reading my Bible, or serving God's people? I learned the importance of pulling away from Satan's suggestions to follow God's direction. After all, Satan is knocking on the door too. But James 4:7 reminds us to submit ourselves, therefore, to God. Resist the devil, and he will flee from you.

Timeout Takeaways

Jesus doesn't want to barge into our lives.

Who's at the door? Don't open the door to strangers. Just like my mother did not open the door until she saw me, we cannot open the door to every distraction. We must be selective about the people and things we allow in our lives. Especially anything that will distract us from spending time with God. Invite Jesus to come into your day through prayer. Make time to read the Bible and meditate on God's word. Don't forget to leave time in your schedule to serve people in need.

Listen for the voice of Christ.

An intimate relationship with Christ requires all the things that help us know Christ better, like prayer, fasting, meditation, and studying God's word. Satan, who comes to steal, kill, and destroy, wants to lure us away from Christ. There are so many distractions in this world that, if we are not careful, they will lull us to sleep to the point where we don't see any need for a closer walk with Jesus.

Be ready for Christ.

Don't ignore Jesus. A committed relationship with Christ involves listening to the voice of God. Connect with God daily through prayer and ask for specific instructions on what you should do to help other people. Look for opportunities to serve God's people through ministries at your local church or in your neighborhood. Offer to help your neighbor with grocery shopping or with yard chores. As the Holy Spirit leads you, use that time together to talk about how knowing Christ has blessed your life.

GRATEFUL

What are you grateful for today?

LISTENING

Ask God to provide clear instructions on how you can deepen your fellowship with Christ.

OBSERVATION

Read Revelation 3:14-22.

WITNESS

Find a person you can talk to about the time Jesus called, and you answered.

DAY 9 - TIME TO BELIEVE

Note to self:

Dear God,

I chose to believe by faith that you are in control. I believe, but please help my unbelief. Once I put doubt and fear out of my mind, I know I can trust your plan. I believe your word is true and that your goodness and mercy shall follow me all of my days. Thank you for the chance to grow in grace.

I have faith to believe.

The others sat there, awestruck. "You really are the Son of God!" they exclaimed.

Matthew 14:33

On my way home from London, I ran into bad weather during my layover in Chicago. As I walked through Chicago's O'Hare airport, I immediately sensed trouble in the air. The airport was overflowing with people. The waiting areas around each gate were full of people sitting in chairs and on the floor. The walls of the airport were lined with people sleeping on the floor or working on their laptop computers and phones. After looking at the Arrivals and Departures board, I soon realized that multiple flights were being delayed or canceled.

While it appeared that every flight to Raleigh, North Carolina, had been canceled or delayed, the gate agent assured me that he would put my name on the waiting list for the next flight out. He told me that if I didn't get on a flight that day, I wouldn't be able to get on another flight for at least 48 hours. Disappointment started to set in. My chances of getting home didn't look too good. I called my husband to tell him the news. After hearing my story, my husband told me to trust God in the storm.

In Matthew 14:22-24, we find the disciples in a storm. After feeding five thousand people with fish and bread, Jesus made the disciples leave the area immediately. At first glance, it might be hard to imagine Jesus sending his disciples away, leaving him alone with the crowd. But Jesus knew what he was doing. He compelled, or as some translations put it, he *made* the disciples get in the boat without him. (v.22) Once the disciples were gone, Jesus sent the crowd home quickly. Jesus did not want the group to take him by force to make him king (John 6:15). With the disciples and the crowd gone, Jesus went to the mountains to pray.

Meanwhile, the disciples were in a boat traveling on the Sea of Galilee. The Sea of Galilee is known for having sudden storms due to its position in the valley. The disciples found themselves in one of those sudden storms. They tried to control the boat during the storm with all their strength, but it was impossible. The boat was now in the middle of the sea, tossed by the waves and contrary winds (Matt. 14:24).

Did Jesus know he was sending the disciples into a storm? Absolutely. The storm was part of God's will for the disciples. Following Christ doesn't always mean "smooth sailing." Storms will come. But Jesus will never leave us to go through the storm alone.

In the fourth watch of the night, between 3 and 6 a.m., Jesus left the mountains. As the disciples struggled to get their boat under control, Jesus appeared to the disciples walking on the sea. But when the disciples saw Jesus, they were afraid and thought he was a ghost. In their time of need, the disciples allowed fear to cloud their focus. When Jesus heard them, he told the disciples to be of good cheer and to not be afraid. (v. 27).

When Peter saw Jesus, he said, "Lord, if it is you, command me to come to You on the water." (v. 28). So Jesus tells Peter to come. Peter gets out of the boat to start walking toward Jesus. But when Peter faced the boisterous wind, he got scared and began to sink. Afraid, Peter cries out, Lord, save me. (v. 30) After Jesus rescues Peter, he speaks to him about his little faith, which led Peter to doubt and fear. Jesus then asks Peter, why did you doubt? (v. 31) In asking the question, Jesus forces Peter to confront his fear.

In the midst of it all, the disciples are still in the boat. Once Peter and Jesus got in the boat, the wind stopped blowing. Everyone in the boat goes from fear to worshipping Jesus until someone says, "You really are the Son of God." (v. 33).

Timeout takeaway

Open your mouth

The Bible offers many beautiful examples of how God hears us during the storms of life. The psalmist in Psalm 107:28 reminds us of the people who had to travel on the ocean. When they ran into stormy wind and waves, they cried to God. Suddenly, God would calm the storm and carry them to their final destination. When life's storms arise, God doesn't want us to weather the storms alone. He wants us to call on him in prayer. While I was at the airport in Chicago, not knowing if I would get home, I started to pray. Not just for a flight home but also for the patience and strength to wait for a plane to take me home. As people were yelling and crying (yes, there were lots of tears that day), I prayed for other people's travel plans. By the time I arrived at the gate, my name was first on the list, and I was going home.

Open your ears

There are two types of storms found in scripture. There are storms of correction where God disciplines us and storms of perfection where God helps us grow. Jonah was in a storm of correction because he disobeyed God. After God initially told Jonah to speak to the people of Nineveh about their wickedness, Jonah refused (Jonah 1:1-3). Instead, he hopped on a ship traveling in the opposite direction to Tarshish. While on the boat, God caused a great storm to arise. But once the men on the ship threw Jonah overboard, the storm stopped (Jonah 1:15). In Matthew 14:22, the disciples were in a storm of perfection because Jesus commanded that they get into the boat. Through the apostles' storm of perfection, we see an example of how Jesus shows up in the midst of a storm. The first thing he said to the apostles was, "Don't be afraid." (v. 27) When we cry out to Jesus, like the apostles did, we must expect to hear his voice. So many times I listen to believers talk about waiting to hear from the Lord before making a decision. But when God speaks, they don't move. I've been guilty of doing the same thing. But we must expect to hear from Christ when he speaks and be willing to move forward according to his instructions. In both types of storms, we must open our ears to listen.

Open your eyes

As the apostles battled the storm in their boat, Jesus started to walk toward them on the water. When they saw Jesus, the apostles thought he was a ghost. They did not see Jesus. So he told them not to worry and not to be afraid. Sometimes as we go through life's storms, it's hard to see that help is on the way. My trip home from London left me feeling stressed. It was hard to see how God would work everything out. But the more I work to build my relationship with God, the better I get at recognizing God's voice. Standing in the airport looking at the list of names on the electronic board, I could slowly see my name going from the bottom to the top. As I described what was going on to my husband, he kept encouraging me to trust God to get me home.

GRATEFUL

What are you grateful for today?

LISTENING

Ask God to provide clear instructions on where he wants you to go this year.

OBSERVATION

Read Matthew 14.

WITNESS

Find a person you can talk to about a time when God brought you out of a storm in your life.

DAY 10 - TIME TO TAKE ANOTHER LOOK

Note to self:

Dear Lord,

Thanks for allowing me to see life through new eyes. I used to think everything in my life had to happen according to my plan. But now I see that your plans for my life are better than anything

I could ask or think. Forgive me for the times I put my trust in the wrong things. I used to trust my accomplishments, my connections, and my employer. No more. I put my trust in you and stand on the promises of your word.

You changed my perspective, and I am so grateful.

DAY 10 - TIME TO TAKE ANOTHER LOOK

That same day two of them were walking to the village Emmaus, about seven miles out of Jerusalem. They were deep in conversation, going over all these things that had happened. In the middle of their talk and questions, Jesus came up and walked along with them. But they were not able to recognize who he was.

Luke 24:13-16

When I was in the third grade, I went to an elementary school three blocks from my grandmother's house. In the mornings, I walked to school with a friend or got a ride. But walking home from school was different. Sometimes I had to walk alone. Not wanting me to walk home by myself, my grandmother told my brother to meet me outside my school so he could walk me home. Each day, my brother would stand in front of a house across the street from my school. As I walked home with my friend, my brother would walk along on the other side of the street.

Do you ever feel like you are alone? Life's challenges, disappointments, or setbacks all have a way of making us feel as if we are moving through life alone. In Luke 24, we find Cleopas and another disciple walking to Emmaus, a town about seven miles from Jerusalem. As they walk along talking about the crucifixion of Jesus Christ, the risen Savior begins walking alongside them. However, the men did not know who Jesus was because they did not recognize him (24:16).

When Jesus asks the men what they are talking about, they could not hide their discouragement (v. 17). Nor could they conceal their shock that the visitor did not know what happened to Jesus over the weekend. Not only did the men try to explain who Jesus was to Jesus, but they revealed something much deeper: the men lost hope. "We were hoping that he would be the one to free Israel." (24:21) Because Jesus was no longer there in the flesh, the men believed he was gone. Ironically, the men thought Jesus left them alone without hope. Their disappointment and unbelief caused them not to recognize Jesus.

How many times have you lost hope? Sometimes when we lose things, like a job, a relationship, or even a loved one, we feel lost. Even those who commit their lives to Christ can sometimes miss seeing him. In all fairness, the men did not expect to see Jesus. Sometimes we only see what we want to see. If all hope is gone, then the only thing we expect to see is trouble. Cleopas and his friend didn't expect Jesus to walk alongside them. But when we commit our lives to God, just like he promised Joshua, God promises never to leave us or forsake us (Deuteronomy 31:6).

Timeout Takeaways

Walk the walk.

In reading Luke chapter 24, we see lots of movement. From the women arriving at the tomb where Jesus's body was laid (v. 1) to the disciples walking along the road to Emmaus, we see that life is not static. God's people are expected to move. More importantly, when we give our lives to Christ, we are expected to move according to God's Spirit. If we allow him, God will lead and guide us through his Holy Spirit. Even during periods when God changes the pace of our lives, we must move according to God's instructions. After being laid off from working in a corporate environment, God didn't tell me to go home and feel sorry for myself. He called me to continue serving his people through my local church and in my community. Throughout our life and our walk with Christ, we cannot allow circumstances to prevent us from seeing Christ walking alongside us.

Take another look.

Why couldn't Cleopas and his friend see Jesus? It's easy to think they were blinded on purpose until verse 25:

> Then Jesus said to the two men, "You are foolish and slow to realize what is true. You should believe everything the prophets said."

Jesus reminded the men of how the prophets and the scriptures detailed the need for the Messiah's crucifixion. So why couldn't the men see Jesus? They did not believe all that the prophets wrote in the scriptures. (v. 25) Despite reading God's word or hearing the preached word, we sometimes fail to believe.

Without the belief that God can and will deliver us from our darkest hour, we mistakenly believe we walk alone. Once we recognize we have been deceived by unbelief, we must be like the father who asked Jesus to help save his son. Jesus said to the father, "Why did you say, 'if you can'? All things are possible for the one who believes." Immediately the father shouted, "I do believe. Help me to believe more!" (Mark 9:23-24) When we take another look, we must believe we will see Christ.

Expect to see more.

By the time Jesus and the two disciples reached Emmaus, Jesus acted as if he planned to continue on his way, but the men begged him to stay. Once their eyes were open, they could see

Jesus. Cleopas and his friend asked Jesus to stay with them, and he accepted their invitation (v. 29). The more the two disciples listened to Jesus, the more everything made sense to them. When we open our eyes, we can see God working. Change may not happen all at once, but we can believe that God will not leave or forsake us.

GRATEFUL

What are you grateful for today?

LISTENING

Ask God to show you an area of your life where you can improve your relationship with him.

OBSERVATION

Read Luke 24.

WITNESS

Find a person you can talk to about a time when God opened your eyes to something going on in your life.

Note to self:

Good morning, Heavenly Father,

Thanks for letting me see the start of a brand new day. Order my steps today, Lord. Let my feet walk in the places where you want me to go. I know there have been times when you asked me to go on a mission with you, and I didn't. Forgive me, Lord. I renew my commitment to you today to go where you want me to go. Use my feet to help those in need.

Thank you for being the lifter.

DAY 11 — TIME TO STOP BEING LAME

But Peter said, "We don't have any money for you! But I'll give you something else! I command you in the name of Jesus Christ of Nazareth, walk!"

Acts 3:6

For a brief time after my first job layoff, I worked as a temp. My job was to assist a product manager in organizing and delivering training classes for the sales team. It was a great job in part because of my manager. He was smart, lots of fun, and very gracious in how he recognized my work. He would often send my husband and me to expensive restaurants with instructions to ask for the manager. When we asked for the manager, we were to say, "Randy sent us." Once the restaurant managers realized Randy sent us, they rolled out the red carpet. At these fine establishments, Randy's name carried weight.

Because Jesus's name is the name above all names (Phil 2:9), it carries authority and power. In Acts 2:43, the apostles performed many signs and wonders. Acts 3 and 4 highlight the significance of using the name of the Lord, Jesus Christ. Acts 3 offers a specific example when Peter and John encounter a lame man.

Peter and John arrived at the temple at 3 p.m for daily prayer. As they were going inside, Peter noticed the lame man sitting outside the gate called Beautiful. Because the gate was Corinthian bronze, it gave off a gold appearance. We can only imagine the many people moving around the temple, including other beggars beside the lame man. Every day, the lame man's friends carried him to the gate and left him there to beg. But on this day, the Spirit of God touched Peter's heart to notice the man sitting outside the gate. Like he had done so many times before, the lame man asked Peter and John for money.

Immediately, Peter said, "Look at us!" (v. 5) Certain the two men would give him the money he wanted; the lame man gave Peter and John his undivided attention. But Peter said, "We don't have any money for you (v. 6) Since Acts 2:44-45 describes how the believers pulled their money and resources together to give to those in need, it was not hard to see how Peter and John didn't have any money when the lame man asked. But Peter knew the lame man needed more than money. So Peter used the authority of Jesus's name to say, "But I'll give you something else! I command you in the name of Jesus Christ of Nazareth, walk!" (v. 6)

Not only did Peter speak, but he touched the man by taking his right hand to lift him (v. 7). The man's feet and legs immediately became strong enough for him to start walking, jumping, and praising. No longer lame, the man walked into the temple area with Peter and John. Immediately, everyone recognized the man. People were shocked to see the once lame man now walking. During all the excitement, people ran to Peter and John. Peter immediately let everyone know, "God did it!" (v. 13). He also told the people, "This crippled man was healed because we trusted in Jesus." (v. 16). The man was made well because of faith in Jesus.

Timeout Takeaways

Walk by faith.

The Bible tells us to walk by faith, not by sight (2 Cor 5:7). When Peter tells the lame man to walk, he doesn't hesitate. The man could have said, "I didn't ask to walk; I asked for money." When Peter reached out to take the man's right hand to help lift him to his feet, the man didn't withdraw his hand or say, "I don't want your hand; I asked for money." As Peter helped the man to his feet, the man's feet and legs became strong. In verse 16, Peter tells the people who crowded around them, "This crippled man was healed because we trusted in Jesus." Peter didn't say only the man trusted in Jesus; he said that he and John put their trust in Jesus too. Peter encouraged people to change their hearts and lives. He told the people that once they returned to God, he would not only forgive them of their sins, but he would give them times of spiritual rest. (v. 20)

Walk away from lameness.

Using the power of the name of Jesus, the lame man was able to walk. Up to this point, the man would lay outside the temple begging for money. When he was able to walk, the man went into the temple area walking, jumping, and praising God (v. 8). Lameness refers to an inability to use one or more limbs properly. We may never experience what it's like not to be able to walk physically. But there are times in our lives when we experience spiritual lameness. There have been times when I was disconnected from God. I sat around only asking for what I wanted but not trusting God to give me what I needed. I suffered from spiritual lameness, and I only got better once I trusted God to lift me out of my situation.

Walk with a pep in your step.

When God lifts us out of our crippling situation, we have a new walk. Once the man was on his feet, he jumped up and started to walk. In addition to walking, the man was not ashamed to praise God. So many times, God has brought me out of debilitating situations — bad relationships, financial failures, unfulfilling jobs. After every experience, I have learned to walk a little differently to my next destination.

GRATEFUL

What are you grateful for today?

LISTENING

Ask God to show you where you can improve your walk with him.

OBSERVATION

Read Acts 3.

WITNESS

Tell at least one person about a time when Jesus rescued you.

Note to self:

Good Morning, Lord!

Thank you for reminding me of the story of Peter in prison. I love how there is so much to learn in that story. Every time I read how Peter shows up at the home where people were praying for him, I laugh. There's a William McDowell song about this story that reminds me that nothing happens until something is spoken. You're just waiting to hear our prayers. Forgive me for the times I didn't pray. I've gotten a lot better.

Thank you for answering my prayers.

All the time that Peter was under heavy guard in the jailhouse, the church prayed for him most strenuously.

Acts 12:5

After traveling on business for a week in Italy, my husband and son met me in Milan. Before heading back to the U.S., we traveled by train to Rome for a weekend of sightseeing. When we arrived in Rome at the Termini Train Station, we asked a police officer how to get to the Hotel Artemide.

69

When he told us it was only a ten-minute walk from the station to the hotel, my husband convinced me we should walk. We departed the train station carrying backpacks and pulling our suitcases. After nearly 30 minutes of walking around in the hot summer sun, we still hadn't found the hotel. By this time, we were hot, sweaty, and getting frustrated. While walking, I started to pray and ask God to lead us. As soon as I said, 'amen,' we turned the corner, and I saw the sign for the hotel. God answered my prayer in an instant.

In Acts 12, we find King Herod on a rampage against people who belonged to the church. Not only did King Herod order James to be killed with a sword, but he also had Peter thrown in jail during the Festival of Unleavened Bread. Since he saw how pleased the unbelieving Jews were when they witnessed James being killed, he decided he would do the same to Peter after the Passover. But the wicked ruler underestimated the power of prayer.

While Peter was in jail, the church prayed to God for him (v. 5). During his time in prison, Peter was guarded by a group of 16 soldiers. While asleep and chained to two soldiers, an angel tapped Peter on the side and woke him up. When the angel said, "Hurry, get up!" the chains fell off Peter's hands (v. 7). Peter continued to follow instructions as the angel told him to put on his clothes, sandals, and coat before leaving the jail cell. Despite thinking the angel was just a vision, Peter continued following the

70

angel past two guards. When they walked a block past the iron gate that separated them from the clty, the angel left Peter. At that moment, Peter realized what happened and thought, "Now I know that the Lord sent his angel to me. He rescued me from Herod, and from everything those Jews thought would happen to me." (v. 11)

A free man, Peter, went to Mary's home, John's mother. This was the home where the believers met to pray for his release from prison. When Rhoda answered the door, she recognized Peter's voice, and she was happy. So happy that she forgot to open the door. She ran inside and told the group, "Peter is at the door!" (v. 14) Have you ever prayed for something, and then when God answered your prayer, you couldn't believe it? Well, that's how the believers at Mary's house reacted as they said to her, "You are crazy!" (v. 15) As Peter continued to knock, the believers opened the door to see Peter standing there (v. 16). Just like that, their prayers had been answered.

Everyone wants God to hear their prayers. The Psalms offer several examples where David and other psalmists prayed, cried, or whispered to God. "Hear my prayer" (4:1), my voice (5:3), my cry (77:1), my groans (102:20). In Psalm 55:1-2, David said, "Open your ears, God, to my prayer; don't pretend you don't hear me knocking. Come close and whisper your answer. I need you." No matter where we are, God will lean in to hear our prayers, even if they are prayers like the one I prayed on the streets of Rome where "My heart meditated, and my spirit asked." (Psalm 77:6). All we have to do is say the word, and God is ready to listen.

Timeout Takeaways

Prayer can break chains.

From the time Peter was thrown in prison, the church started praying passionately for his release (v. 5). Peter was bound with two chains, peacefully asleep between two soldiers (v. 6). Peter was on lockdown and not going anywhere. But when the angel of the Lord showed up in Peter's cell, his chains fell off (v. 7). Prayer can break chains. However, sometimes when we have a problem, we do everything except but pray. Rather than being weighed down by life's challenges, we must go to God in prayer.

Prayer can open doors.

The angel led Peter past the first guard and then the second before coming to an iron gate that led into the city. The gate swung open on its own. Once they reached the first intersection, the angel left Peter, and that's when he realized he was not dreaming. Peter said, "I can't believe it—this happened! The Master sent his angel and rescued me from Herod's vicious little production and the spectacle the Jewish mob was looking forward to." (v.11) Even Peter had a hard time believing that God stepped in so quickly. However, he did not hesitate to move through each open door.

Prayer can blow your mind.

Still amazed at how God got him out of prison, Peter goes to Mary's house where everyone met to pray. When Peter knocked on the door, everyone was shocked. After leaving him standing outside for a while, they finally let Peter in, and he told them what happened. Everyone was amazed at what God did for Peter. Through prayer, God can blow your mind.

GRATEFUL

What are you grateful for today? How will you respond with gratitude to any change currently happening in your life?

LISTENING

Through prayer, ask God to reveal any sin that has you in bondage.

OBSERVATION

Read Acts 12.

WITNESS

Talk to someone about a time when you prayed, and God delivered you from a challenging situation.

DAY 13 - TIME TO COME OUT OF THE WILDERNESS

Note to self:

Good Morning, Lord!

I woke up this morning at peace. I can remember a time when I woke up feeling anxious and weighed down with worry and fear. No more, thanks to you, Lord. It feels good to wake up, surrounded by your peace and love. Please forgive me for the life I once lived. Please help me never to forget that I can find strength in you.

I am a survivor.

DAY 13 - TIME TO COME OUT OF THE WILDERNESS

Then Jesus was led out into the wilderness by the Holy Spirit, to be tempted there by Satan. ² For forty days and forty nights he ate nothing and became very hungry.

¹⁰ "Get out of here, Satan," Jesus told him. "The Scriptures say, 'Worship only the Lord God. Obey only him.'"

¹¹ Then Satan went away, and angels came and cared for Jesus.

Matthew 4:1-2, 10-11

It's easy to feel challenged when our lives get knocked off course. One minute your career is going smoothly, and the next minute you're standing in the unemployment office. One day you're engaged to be married, and the next day the wedding is off. Moments like this can leave us feeling lost in the wilderness.

In his book titled *Wilderness Survival*, Gregory Davenport believes the three steps to wilderness survival are the will to survive, equipment, and survival knowledge. As someone determined to survive my last job layoff, I equipped myself with prayer and the Bible as I read Matthew 4 to find out how Jesus survived his wilderness experience.

Jesus was led by the Spirit into the wilderness to be tempted by the devil (v. 1). Not because God wanted to see if Jesus would resist Satan. Jesus went through a wilderness experience to expose Satan's tricks and to show every believer how to survive. Jesus faced Satan as a man and showed us how to depend on the Holy Spirit's power.

In his first attempt, Satan said, "If thou be the Son of God, command that these stones be made bread. (v. 3) Satan attempts to call into question the love God has for his children. If you are the Son of God, then why are you here in this wilderness? Next, Satan suggests that Jesus take care of his own needs by turning the bread into stone. How many times has this happened in your life? God isn't moving fast enough, so the enemy strikes fear in your heart, and you decide to handle it yourself. Jesus shows us how to resist Satan's trick by saying, "'It is not just bread that keeps people alive. Their lives depend on what God says.'" (v. 4) Jesus's response relates to Deuteronomy 8:3 where we see God's word is what we need to keep us going during tough times.

In his second attempt, Satan uses God's word in tempting Christ. "If you are the Son of God, jump off, because the Scriptures say, 'God will command his angels to help you, and their hands will catch you so that you will not hit your foot on a rock.'" (v. 6). By saying, "It is written" in verse 4 and "It is written again," in verse 7, Jesus lets the enemy know that he takes his direction from the word of God. Like Jesus, we must trust God completely rather than depending on our knowledge (Proverbs 3:5). Jesus did not fall for Satan' trick to twist God's word, so Jesus let Satan know that "Thou shalt not tempt the Lord thy God." (v. 7)

The third time Satan tempted Christ, he said, "All these things will I give thee if thou wilt fall and worship me." (v. 9) Satan tried to offer Jesus something that was not his to give: a shortcut to the kingdom. Jesus knew he would have to suffer crucifixion on the cross before he could enter into the glory (Luke 24:26, 1 Peter 1:11). But he also knew that worshipping Satan was not part of the plan. Does God allow Satan to act like the God of this age (2 Corinthians 4:4)? Yes, that authority came through Adam and his descendants' failure to resist the devil. If Satan had his way, everyone would worship him, and he would take God's place (Isaiah 14:12-14). But Jesus puts him in his place by saying two critical things. First, Thou shalt worship the Lord thy God (v. 10a). Second, Jesus tells Satan that God is the only one to be served.

Timeout Takeaways

The love of God.

Satan wants us to doubt God's love. By saying, "If you are the Son of God," Satan tries to tempt Jesus into using his divine power to change his situation. In Genesis 3, we find a similar approach as the serpent tempts Eve to eat from the tree in the middle of the garden, "You will not die. God knows that if you eat the fruit from that tree, you will learn about good and evil, and then you will be like God!" (v. 4) Looking at both examples, I see how Satan tries to not only invoke doubt and fear but tries to tempt us to ignore God's instructions. God loves us enough to see us through every temptation we face.

The word of God.

Satan wants us to doubt the word of God. In Matthew 4:6, Satan quotes Psalm 91:11-12 when he said, "If you are the Son of God, jump off, because the scriptures say, 'God will command his angels to help you, and their hands will catch you so that you will not hit your foot on a rock.'" But he leaves out a portion of the scripture that states, *in all thy ways*. As believers, we should never try to get God to do something spectacular to prove his love for us. God showed us how much he loved us in Romans 5:8, when Christ died for us.

The will of God.

Satan wants us to ignore the will of God. The enemy offers Jesus a shortcut to all the kingdoms of the world, but only if he agrees to bow down and worship him. (Matthew 4:9) This offer of instant gratification is one that Satan presents to everyone. Satan tempts us to buy things we cannot afford. Think about how many times you were tempted to buy a house, or a car, or clothes you knew you couldn't afford. I cannot tell you how many times I fell into those traps when I was younger. Instead of waiting patiently for God's plan to unfold in my life, I jumped right in. Only to end up trying to work extra hours to make extra money to pay off credit card debt. Before I knew it, Satan had me right where he wanted me -- stressed, worried, and in debt. Giving in to temptation is not God's will for our lives. Instead, we must submit to God, resist the devil, and he will flee (James 4:7)

GRATEFUL

What are you grateful for today?

LISTENING

Ask God to show you how to deal with your wilderness experiences.

OBSERVATION

Read Matthew 4.

WITNESS

Talk to someone about a time when you faced temptation and how God delivered you.

DAY 14 - TIME TO LISTEN

Note to self:

Thank you, Lord, for waking me up today. I enjoy our time together in the mornings. I know the enemy wants me to believe everything is more important than spending time with you, God. Forgive me for all the times I fell for that lie. I know now that spending time reading your word and praying in the mornings is the best way to start every day. Now that you and I have been together this morning, I'm ready to take on the day.

Lead me on.

"Oh yes, Judgment Day is coming!"

These are the words of my Master God.

"I'll send a famine through the whole country.

It won't be food or water that's lacking, but my word.

Amos 8:11

When a lethal virus wipes out the grass of the earth, in the book, *The Death of Grass*, chaos ensues. Apart from grass, in this science fiction thriller, wheat, barley, peas, rice, and rye are all wiped out by the virus. Governments and scientists work to create a counter-virus in a race against time. Before the planet goes into drought, it's only a matter of time. The world's food supply is scarce as people struggle to survive.

Unlike the story we find in *The Death of Grass*, the Book of Amos describes a different famine type. "The time is surely coming," says the Lord God, "when I will send a famine on the land—not a famine of bread or water, but of hearing the words of the Lord. (Amos 8:11) During this peculiar time, there will not be a famine of the word of God, but a famine of hearing God's words.

80

his word will still be available and accessible, but no one will hear God's words because of a curse on the land. In the same way, God can withhold the rain (Amos 4:7), he can also withhold his words.

So what led God to this decision? During this time, both Israel and Judah experienced prosperity and military success. For example, Samaria, the capital city of Israel, was a place of wealth and luxury. Unfortunately, some people living there lived immorally and practiced idolatry. While the leaders in the town enjoyed prosperity, the poor did not.

God called Amos, a sheep breeder, to leave his flock and speak against Samaria's evil and self-indulgence. Specifically, the prophecy of Amos was intended for the people in the northern kingdom of Israel. God showed Amos a series of visions. In chapter eight, Amos sees a basket of ripe summer fruit, which suggests the end of a growth cycle from seed to harvest. When Amos tells God what he sees, God said, "The end has come to my people Israel. I will not ignore their sins anymore. (v. 2) It was clear that Israel was ripe for judgment as they mistreated the needy and cheated people using dishonest scales (8:4-5). God's decision would be destructive (8:8-13).

Therefore, the "hearing" referred to in Amos 8:11 is more than mere words. Instead, it is the hearing that involves focused attention on God's words that result in obedience. The type of famine that God describes would leave people without direction or focus to make the right decisions.

Ultimately, sin and disobedience would flourish. Without God's words as guidance, the nation would stumble around without the light of truth. Sadly, there would be many who wouldn't recognize the real curse in not hearing God's words. At the same time, others who have gotten used to going without hearing the truth from God may seem relieved. But divine instruction is essential.

God wants his people to be obedient and to be a blessing. He expects believers to pass blessings on to others as he extends blessings to them. As part of the design of heaven, enjoying God's blessings is not enough. Each believer has to be ready to live generously.

Despite the judgment described in Amos, God also promises restoration to a remnant of Israel. About King David's lineage, God said he would restore David's house that has fallen to pieces. God promises to repair the holes in the roof, replace the broken windows, and fix it up like new. (Amos 9:11) This blessing will not only be extended to the Davidic monarchy but everyone under it plus everyone else under God's sovereign judgment. (v. 12)

Timeout Takeaways

Open your ears to hear God speak.

God wants to share his word with his people. God's word is full of invitations to call on him. Jeremiah 33:3 is an example: Call to me and I will answer you and will tell you great and hidden things that you have not known. But he doesn't want his words to fall on deaf ears. How would you like it if you always shared your wisdom and knowledge with your children only to have them ignore you? When we neglect to hear God, spiritual deafness can set in where we hear God, but we never follow his instructions. God promises blessings to those who listen to him and obey his word. But he said, "Blessed rather are those who hear the word of God and keep it!" (Luke 11:28)

Open your heart to obedience.

God doesn't want his children to love the world more than they love him (1 John 2:15). Loving the world means pleasing our sinful selves, either through the wicked things we see or being proud of what we have (1 John 2:16). But once we surrender our lives to Christ, we must let worldly desires go. Whoever does what God wants will live forever (1 John 2:17). Therefore, every believer must follow Jesus's example of obedience, "but I do as the Father has commanded me, so that the world may know that I love the Father." (John 14:31)

Open your arms to God's blessings.

Part of God's anger with Samaria in the Amos 8 came because of their sinfulness and self-indulgence. Through Amos, God wanted people to know that rebellion against him would not result in kingdom blessings, despite prosperity. When the Holy Spirit opens our eyes to anything that leads us away from obedience, we must change. God's blessings come to those who obey him and who follow his voice.

GRATEFUL

What are you grateful for today?

LISTENING

Ask God what he would like you to do after reading this devotional.

OBSERVATION

Read Amos 8.

WITNESS

Talk to someone about when you heard the voice of the Lord and what he asked you to do.

The interview went great, and I thought I would get a job offer. But when the recruiter told me they offered the job to someone else, I was so disappointed.

How many times were you passed over for a job or an assignment you thought was perfect for you? You had it all worked out in your mind: You would go to the interview, dazzle the hiring manager with your experience, and walk away with a new job or assignment that would look great on your resume. But in the end, you didn't get the job.

I know how that must have felt. Early in my career, I can remember finding what I thought was the perfect job, and applying for it, only to find out someone else got the job. I couldn't help thinking, "I wanted that job. It was perfect for me." I was so disappointed.

When I think back to every job or assignment I applied for, there was always a sense of worry. Have I done enough in my career to prove I am deserving of this opportunity? Will they like me? Will they see how valuable I could be for the team? Will they pick me? As time moved on, I didn't get selected for a lot of jobs or assignments. Frustrated and tired of being disappointed, I decided to change my approach by letting God take control.

I relied on several scriptures but focused on Philippians 4:6-7:

Do not be anxious about anything, but in everything by prayer and supplication with Thanksgiving, let your requests be known, made known to God, and the peace of God, which surpasses all understanding, will guard your hearts and your minds in Christ Jesus.

I love Philippians 4:6-7 because it turned out to be what I needed to deal with life's disappointments and to stop worrying. Once I spent time meditating on and studying this scripture, I realized that God never wanted me to have the jobs or assignments I didn't get. If I am prepared to trust God to open doors, I must trust him to keep some doors closed. As it turns out, one of the jobs I applied for ended a year later, leaving the person in the position without a job. Today, I pray and ask God to lead me to the assignments he wants me to take. If I get an offer, I thank God, and if I don't get an offer, I thank God.

The beautiful thing about God is that he sees what we can't see. He knows which doors he wants us to stay away from and which doors he wants us to walk through. If you find yourself repeatedly feeling frustrated and disappointed, here are a few things you can try:

Make a list of the reasons you want the new job or assignment. Use your journal to write down why it's essential for

86

you to get this job. Identify the skills you have and the skills you don't have.

Ask God to speak to your heart about the job. Use prayer and journal writing to talk to God about the job. Ask him if this is the job or assignment he wants you to have, and if not, what would he like you to do instead.

Decide what you will do after the selection has been made. Identify five things you plan to do after a decision about the job or assignment has been made. For example, after I didn't get selected to lead a writing project, I started working on writing projects outside of work.

DAY 15 - TIME TO LOOKUP

Note to self:

Dear Lord,

Thank you for blessing me above all I could ask or think. You have given me so much. Yet, there are times when I know I didn't give you as much of myself as you deserve. Please forgive me for giving so much of my attention to other people and other things while ignoring you and your business. No more. Help me reprioritize my time so I can serve wherever I am needed.

Thank you for helping me see life through new eyes as I reset.

DAY 15 - TIME TO LOOKUP

So if you're serious about living this new resurrection life with Christ, *act* like it. Pursue the things over which Christ presides. Don't shuffle along, eyes to the ground, absorbed with the things right in front of you. Look up, and be alert to what is going on around Christ—that's where the action is. See things from *his* perspective.

Colossians 3:1-2

I decided in 2011 to begin cycling. My husband was already a cyclist, riding between 50 to 100 miles on the weekends. So it was easy for me to learn about the sport of cycling from him. Sometimes, my husband and I, along with our friends, would take our children on Sunday afternoon rides. First, we started out riding three miles, then eight miles, until we worked our way up to more than 20 miles at a time.

After months of training, we decided to sign up for a charity ride. Anyone who wanted to participate in the ride could cycle 17, 35, or 50 miles. My son and I took the 17-mile route. My husband was on the 50-mile route, and my godson and his parents were on the 35-mile route. My son and I started the race with more than

100 riders. But after about five miles, we found ourselves riding alone on the rural highways of Rocky Mount, North Carolina. Not many riders took the 17-mile route.

I didn't think my first charity ride would be like this. I envisioned riding with my family and friends while laughing and enjoying the beautiful North Carolina sun. Instead, I was riding alone on rural highways, past barns and cows with my seven-year-old son.

Concerned, my son said, "How will we know which way to go?" I explained that we would have to focus on the colored mile markers painted on the ground, specifically for the charity ride. I asked him if he remembered where the starting line was, and he did. After explaining that the starting line would also be the finish line, I told him to 'Focus on the finish.'

In Colossians 3, Paul lets us know where we should focus our attention. Paul writes a letter to a church that has slowed down its worship. He reminds the church members that they not only died with Christ, but they were raised with Christ, too. When Christ rose from the dead, he was raised to sit next to God in heaven. For this reason, Paul encourages believers to live for what is in heaven because that's where Christ sits (v. 2). Since Christ's believers share his risen life, our interests and attention should focus on Christ.

But it's easy to get distracted. If we are not careful, distractions will cause us to lose our focus on Christ. Have you ever been so consumed with a work project that you couldn't help out at church? Have you ever been so engrossed in going to school that you stopped going to church so you could do your homework? I have talked to lots of believers who love Christ but fall into this trap. Everything in the life of a Christian must be prioritized, including our thoughts. By setting our minds on the things above, we discipline ourselves to focus on what's important in building God's kingdom.

Timeout Takeaways

A disciplined mind requires training.

Before my son and I entered the charity ride, we trained. On our Sunday rides, we would cycle around 16 to 18 miles. As an incentive for the children, we would stop for ice cream at a local McDonald's conveniently located off the trail where we trained. To take earthly action, we must train our minds to focus on heavenly things. Consistent personal and corporate Bible study time, daily prayer, and private fasting are ways to train our minds to focus on Christ.

Victorious living requires a shift in focus.

During the charity ride, I was concerned my son would become bored and want to quit in the middle of nowhere. Plus, I didn't want him to worry about being separated from the other riders. I had to get him to shift his focus to one of his favorite subjects: superheroes. While riding along the quiet countryside, Cole told me everything I ever wanted to know about The Flash — how he got his powers, who his enemies were, how his dad ended up in jail, and so on. Before I knew it, we were at the finish line. If every follower of Christ is to be victorious, we must shift our focus to look at heaven's perspective on how to live.

A new identity requires a new mentality.

Paul reminds us that when we accepted Christ, we died. Our old life shouldn't have the same power over us. I can remember when I always tried to read the Bible at the end of the day. Most days were long and exhausting, and I often fell asleep after reading one or two verses. This approach got me nowhere, so I had to make a change. To get into a new routine, I moved my Bible study time to early mornings before going to the gym. At the start of the day, I have more energy and better focus. I became disciplined about spending time with God.

GRATEFUL

What are you grateful for today?

LISTENING

Ask God to show you how to make time in your schedule to meet with him daily.

OBSERVATION

Read Colossians 3.

WITNESS

Talk to someone about how you make time to meet God.

Note to self:

Dear Lord,

Thanks for being with me wherever I go. In the last few years, I experienced some challenges in my career. But in the midst of it all, I got stronger and more resilient. Thanks to you, I adapted and overcame every obstacle. I have a new outlook on life. I am grateful for the goodness and mercy that follows me.

Ready for whatever comes my way.

Have I not commanded you? Be strong and courageous. Do not be frightened, and do not be dismayed, for the Lord your God is with you wherever you go."

Joshua 1:9

In 1995, I worked for a small software company. It was a great job because it allowed me to design a brand new communications department. Because the company was small, I was fortunate to work with leaders in every department. One day, I attended a confidential meeting with the head of the Human Resource department. During our meeting, I learned the company would need to lay off several people. As a result, I would need to write all of the materials needed to share the news with employees and the press.

Although I had experience writing these materials for a past employer, I always asked God to give me strength and wisdom. By the end of the week, I helped the HR director deliver nearly all of the layoff notices to the employees affected by the news. But I could tell she was having difficulty delivering the news to one more person: me. It didn't take me long to realize I was going to get laid off with everyone else. Rather than being angry or scared, I prayed. I asked God to give me the strength to receive the news with grace and peace.

On Friday, I noticed the HR director kept avoiding me. Around 1 p.m. I decided to go to her office. She was sitting at her desk, looking tired and unhappy. When knocked on the door, she looked up. "Can I come in?" I asked. With sadness in her eyes, she said, "Sure." I could see how difficult this day was for her, so I said, "Is there anything you want to talk to me about?" After letting out a big sigh, she said, "Oh, Karen, I hate to do this to you." I immediately told her I understood and that I would be okay. I let her know about my faith in God and that my prayer is that she would have the strength to move forward. She let out another sigh, but this time in relief.

Joshua understood the importance of having faith in God's plan. Out of the 12 spies sent into the promised land, Joshua and Caleb came back with an encouraging report. The other ten spies came back with bad news and caused division among the people. They did not trust where God was leading the people of Israel. As a result, the men whom Moses sent to spy out the land died by the plague before the Lord. (Numbers 14:36-37) Of the 12 spies, only Joshua and Caleb remained alive. (Numbers 14: 38)

When Moses died, God told Joshua to possess the land. In Joshua 1, God said, "Be strong and courageous," in verses 6, 7, and 9. Can you imagine how Joshua must have felt? He's not only about to carry out God's commandment, but he's going with absolute certainty that God's going to be with him. God gives Joshua futher instructions in verse 8:

94

This Book of the Law shall not depart from your mouth, but you shall meditate in it day and night, that you may observe to do according to all that is written in it. For then, you will make your way prosperous, and then you will have success.

As believers our goal should be to take God's word with us wherever we go. The word of God is living and active and sharper than any two-edged sword (Hebrews 4:12), so it makes sense to take God's word along our journey.

Timeout Takeaways

Take on God's confidence.

I firmly believe that challenges can bring change for the better. Through every chapter of our lives, God wants us to be strong and courageous. The enemy wants us to give in to fear and worry. Since giving my life to Christ when I was 16, I have experienced many ups and downs. Throughout the years, I learned to trust where God leads me. I may not always know exactly where I'm going, but I know that God has the perfect plan for me. Let us then, with confidence, draw near to the throne of grace, that we may receive mercy and find grace to help in time of need. (Hebrews 4:12)

Take on God's presence.

God sent Joshua to claim the land he promised. When God takes us to new territory, we need to walk in with a new strategy. If we plan to take on God's presence, we must take on his word. But just like God told Joshua he would be with him, we can count on God being with us when we finally arrive in the place where he told us to go. You make known to me the path of life; in your presence, there is fullness of joy; at your right hand are pleasures forevermore. (Psalm 16:11)

Take on God's promises.

Reject the lies from the enemy. The enemy wants us to be afraid to walk into new territory; he wants us to fear the unknown. The devil is always going to be the same. He comes to steal, kill, and destroy; that's all he knows how to do. Conversely, God is the same yesterday, today, and forever. Because the enemy expects us to be sad about losing things, we must praise God. Because the enemy expects us to be angry when we don't get what we think we deserve, we must accept God's decision. Because the enemy wants us to be afraid of new things, we have to embrace the newness of life. Even if we cannot see what God is doing, it's okay to be fine with not knowing. Fear not, for I am with you; be not dismayed, for I am your God; I will strengthen you, I will help you, I will uphold you with my righteous right hand. (Isaiah 41:10)

GRATEFUL

What are you grateful for today?

LISTENING

Ask God to show you any new places or things he would like you to embrace as part of his plan.

OBSERVATION

Read Joshua 1.

WITNESS

Talk to someone about a time when you trusted God enough to follow his plan for your life.

DAY 17 - TIME TO WALK THROUGH OPEN DOORS

Note to self:

Good Morning, Lord!

Thank you for the hidden treasures you have waiting for me. Because your plan is so much better than mine, I'm expecting explosive blessings in my life. You have done so many things already that I cannot thank you enough. Forgive me for praying but not believing anything would change in my life. Today, I walk by faith and not by sight. Please help me to show others the way that leads to you. I'm excited to see what doors you open for me next.

Thank you in advance.

DAY 17 - TIME TO WALK THROUGH OPEN DOORS

At the same time, pray also for us, that God may open to us a door for the word, to declare the mystery of Christ, on account of which I am in prison.

Colossians 4:3

One of the hardest things I had to hear was, "Your son has a heart defect." Within a few hours of being born, the doctors and nurses took my baby to an examination room where they discovered he had four heart defects. Formerly known as Tetralogy of Fallot, this rare condition causes oxygen-poor blood to flow out of the heart to the rest of the body. Some of the symptoms we witnessed were blue-tinged skin and shortness of breath. At ten-weeks old, Cole needed open-heart surgery.

My husband and I spent a lot of time sitting and praying in doctor's offices and hospital waiting rooms. One day, while waiting to hear an update on Cole's surgery, my husband and I noticed a young couple walk into the waiting room. They were visibly upset. Based on what we heard them say, their son was sick too. Wanting to comfort the young couple, my husband and I shared our story about our son. They were amazed our children were in similar situations. But instead of only focusing on the challenges of having a sick child, we decided to share our faith. God opened the door for us to tell the couple about Jesus Christ.

Paul always looked for opportunities to tell people about Jesus Christ. In Colossians 4:3, he asked his brothers and sisters in Christ in Colossae to pray that doors would open for him to share the gospel with unbelievers. The same image of an open door as an open opportunity for the gospel is seen in Acts 14:27, 1 Corinthians 16:9, and 2 Corinthians 2:12.

In Acts 16, Paul and Silas were beaten and thrown into jail (16:16-25). At midnight, Paul and Silas were singing loudly to God when an earthquake came and opened all the prison doors (v. 26). When the jailer woke up to find all the prison doors opened, he thought all of the prisoners were gone. Since Roman guards faced the same penalty as their escaped prisoners, the jailer took out his sword to kill himself. But Paul stopped him, saying, "Don't do that! We're all still here! Nobody's run away." (v. 28)

Once the jailer had light to see, he brought Paul and Silas out. Once they were outside, the jailer asked Paul and Silas, "Sirs, what do I have to do to be saved, to live?" (v. 29) Paul and Silas told the jailer to "Put your entire trust in the Master Jesus." (v. 31).

The jailer took Paul and Silas to his home, where he cleaned their wounds. Paul and Silas spent the night telling the jailer and his family about Jesus Christ. They wanted to share everything they could about Christ. By the morning, they baptized the jailer and his family. And to think, all of this happened after God opened the door.

God holds the key to every door. He has the power to open or close any door he chooses. For believers, it should be just as easy to celebrate an open door that leads to promotion or recognition as it is to embrace an open door that leads to spreading the gospel of Jesus Christ. After all, Jesus tells us he is the door of the sheep (John 10:7). In sheep farming, the shepherd laid across the sheep pen opening to keep the sheep in and wolves out.

If God opens the door to spread the gospel to someone who does not know him, then the redeemed of the Lord should be the first to speak up. If God has brought you out of darkness into his marvelous light, then you should take advantage of the opportunity to tell others about your experience. If God opens a door that allows you to share your testimony with others, It's time for you to walk through every open door you see.

Timeout Takeaways

God opens doors that lead to rest.

God wants everyone to turn from sin and surrender their life to Christ. God doesn't want anyone lost. He's giving everyone space and time to change (2 Peter 3:9). Therefore, he uses people to tell the world about the saving grace of Jesus Christ. Paul understood this truth. In 1 Corinthians 3, Paul describes how people come to know God. He said that he planted the seed, and Apollos watered it, but God made it grow. (v. 6) For those ready to commit their lives to God, Jesus says, "Come to Me, all who are weary and heavy-laden, and I will give you rest." (Matthew 11:28) From there, Christ invites every believer to accept his teachings and learn from him (Matthew 11:29). As the Lord continues to open my eyes, I see that an open door to Christ leads to rest and his saving grace.

God opens doors that lead to opportunity.

The opportunity to lead others to Christ is not reserved for special people like pastors, deacons, or ministers. All believers are expected to live out God's mission through their daily lives and share the gospel with others. So when God opens the door to the heart of an unbeliever, we have an opportunity and an obligation to tell others about Christ. Paul looked for a chance to share the gospel whenever he could. Despite being a prisoner, Paul didn't hesitate to tell the jailer on how he could be saved. We live with and around people in need of redemption and reconciliation with God. Therefore, every believer must intentionally share the gospel of Jesus Christ with family, friends, and the community.

God opens doors that lead to mission.

Once you give your life to Christ, you officially join God's mission. As disciples, God asks us to make disciples of all nations (Matthew 28:19). *Missio Dei* is the Latin Christian theological term which means "mission of God" or "the sending of God." *Missio Dei* comes from God's very nature because the mission is an attribute of God rather than merely the church's activity. The classical doctrine of *missio Dei* is based on the Trinity – Father, Son, and Holy Spirit – sending the church into the world as an extension of God. Because God is a missionary God, the mission is a movement from God to the world, and the church acts as an instrument for the mission. As we build our relationship with God, it is important to remember that his mission should be our mission.

GRATEFUL

What are you grateful for today?

LISTENING

Ask God to show you how to share his message with others.

OBSERVATION

Read Colossians 4.

WITNESS

Talk to someone about the time when you gave your life to Christ.

DAY 18 - TIME TO COME TO LIFE

Note to Self:

Good Morning, Heavenly Father,

Lord, Thank you for the breath of life. There were many times when I felt dead inside and didn't know if I could go on. Then there were the times when the enemy tried to scare the life out of me.

Forgive me, Lord, for not running to you sooner, Lord. Today, I'm alive and breathing because you didn't give up on me. I'm so grateful for my new life.

This is what the Lord God says to you: I will cause breath to come into you, and you will come to life!

Ezekiel 37:5

The days leading up to Christmas break were always a mad dash. I always had final exams from Monday until Friday. One year, in preparation for going home for two weeks, I attempted to take care of a few things before I left. After the holidays, I wanted to slip back into my college life and start the new year off on the right foot. Before I left, I knew I needed to pay bills, clean out the refrigerator, and I ask my boss, who was really like a mom, to take care of my plants. My boss-mom, Pat, treated me like one of her children. Since Pat and I had previous conversations about me leaving plants unattended and bills unpaid before leaving town, she would ask, "Did you do this or that? Is there anything you need me to do?" She was the best.

By the time Friday rolled around, I was desperate to get on the road for my two and half hour drive home. Pressed for time, I left a few things undone. I stopped by work to pick up my paycheck. I gave my boss-mom a big hug and told her not to worry about the plants. I assured her I gave the plants extra water and that everything would be fine. I was off for two weeks of home-cooked meals and lots of sleep.

At the start of the new year, I returned to Morgantown, West Virginia. When I opened the door to my one-bedroom apartment, everything seemed in order. After putting away the food my mom packed for me, I sat down to watch television, and that's when I saw it: my plants were dead. I shook my head in disappointment. All I had to do was leave the plants with Pat, and none of this would have happened. I remember thinking to myself, 'Karen, when will you learn to listen?'

Israel had a listening problem, which led to destruction and exile. After the Babylonians destroyed Jerusalem, its people, along with the prophet Ezekiel, went into exile in 597 B.C. During this time, Ezekiel was obedient in doing what God asked. In addition to speaking to mountains (6:2, 36:1), and the forest (20:47), God told Ezekiel to prophesy to a valley of dry bones (37:1).

After the hand of the Lord came upon Ezekiel, he found himself in the Spirit of the Lord in a valley full of bones. (37:1) In ancient Israel, exposed remains were a disgrace to the deceased. God warned Israel their sins would lead to shame, "God will defeat you by enemy attack …all the kingdoms of Earth will see you as a horror. Carrion birds and animals will boldly feast on your dead body with no one to chase them away. (Deut 28:25-26, Jeremiah 34:20).

Because the bones were so dry suggested they must have been in the valley a long time. Yet, God asked Ezekiel, "Can these dry bones live?" (v. 3) But Ezekiel didn't doubt God already knew the answer when he said, "Oh Lord God, you know" (v. 3). God tells Ezekiel to speak to the dry bones, 'Dry bones, listen to the Message of God!'" (v. 4) Through Ezekiel, God said he would bring the dry bones to life, and they would recognize him as God. (v. 5-6).

As Ezekiel prophesied, the bones moved and came together with skin stretched over them but without breath. (v. 7-8) Next, God told Ezekiel to prophesy to the breath to, "Breath on these slain bodies. Breath life!" (v. 9) As Ezekiel spoke the words, breath entered the army, and they were suddenly alive. (v. 10)

The vision represented the entire Jewish nation, both Israel and Judah. While Israel's nation will come together, they will not have spiritual life until they see their Messiah, believe in him, and receive the Holy Spirit of God. (Ezekiel, 39:29). Likewise, God's people today are sometimes like the army of bones, life-like but spiritually dead. Sin and disobedience result in a disconnect from God. But as the Spirit of God enters, so should an eagerness to know and obey God.

Timeout Takeaways

Time to obey

With submission and repentance, a caring, devoted relationship with Jesus begins. (Matthew 16:24-27, Acts 2:38) From there, to live a life of faith that is true to God's word, every disciple of Christ must be deliberate. "As obedient children, do not be conformed to the passions of your former ignorance." (1 Peter 1:14)

Time to live

After Ezekiel spoke and the dry bones came together, they still did not have life. God asked Ezekiel to speak to the wind and say, "Wind, come from every direction and breathe air into these dead bodies! Breathe into them, and they will come to life again!" (37:9) In Hebrew, the word *ruah* means "wind, breath, spirit or Spirit." It wasn't until God's Spirit entered the bones that they came to life (37:10). We found this in Genesis 2:7, when God made Adam from dust. Adam didn't come to life until God breathed life into his nostrils. God's Spirit brings life.

Time to flow

Disobedience and sin cause separation from God. Going to church and reading the Bible is not enough to keep us connected to God if we continue to disobey or sin. The wages of sin is death (Romans 6:23). Without God's Spirit and obedience, a believer can suffer from dryness. But to every disciple who thirsts, Jesus promises that "living water shall flow from the inmost being of anyone who believes in me." (John 7:37-38)

GRATEFUL

What are you grateful for today?

LISTENING

Ask God to show you any area of your faith walk that is dead or dried up.

OBSERVATION

Read Ezekiel 37.

WITNESS

Talk to someone about the time when you God refreshed your life.

DAY 19 - TIME FOR A SECOND WIND

Note to self:

Good Morning, Lord!

I am so grateful to be alive and well. Thank you for giving me the strength to make it every day. Even though I am tired from working on my business at the end of the day, I am happy and at peace. With renewed strength, I am ready to tackle everything you have planned for me today.

Please give me focus and direction today. I don't have any time to waste. Show me what I can do and where I should go today to let someone know about your good news.

Ready and willing.

DAY 19 - TIME FOR A SECOND WIND

But they who wait for the Lord shall renew their strength; they shall mount up with wings like eagles; they shall run and not be weary; they shall walk and not faint.

Isaiah 40:31

I decided to make a bold move on July 4, 2012. Not only did I sign up for the 20th Annual Firecracker Race, an annual charity ride in North Carolina, but it was the first time I had clip-in pedals. To enhance pedal strokes, cyclists use clip-in pedals, where their shoe connects to the pedal. My husband kept telling me how much smoother my ride would be if I used clip-in pedals so I decided to see for myself.

I signed up for the 50K route, which is about 31 miles. The race started at 7 a.m., and by 10 a.m., it was 102 degrees in the scorching hot North Carolina sun. By the time I got to mile 28, I was weary, frustrated, and ready to give up. During the last three miles of my 31-mile journey, I had to make it up a steep hill. As people passed me, they said encouraging things like, "You can make it," "Just a little while longer." A man who looked like he was in his 70s came gliding past me and said, "Don't give up, you got this. Just keep going." The man's words of comfort helped me more than he could ever know.

God offers words of comfort in the 40th chapter of Isaiah. It's essential to recognize that the book of Isaiah has three specific themes. Chapters 1-35 are prophetic and focus on condemnation. Chapters 36-39 are historical with a theme of confiscation. Finally, chapters 40-66 are messianic with a theme of consolation. The second half of Isaiah looks ahead to the Babylonian captivity of Judah. Also, chapters 40-66 look forward to the suffering of Jesus the Messiah.

Israel had committed great sins against the Lord. As a result, the Lord punished the people. But God still loved them. Unfortunately, all the people could see were their past sins and failures. They were in desperate need of encouragement. From the start of Isaiah 40, God wanted the people to hear his tender words. (v. 1) God also made it very clear that Israel served her sentence, that her sin was taken care of—forgiven. (v. 2) Through

110

Isaiah, the Jews were told they had been punished enough, and now it's over and done. The people were reminded to, Lift your eyes on high, and behold who hath created these things; he is strong in power (v. 26).

But instead of praising the Lord, the people complained as if God didn't care about their situation. (v. 27) The people seemed to forget that the Lord is the Everlasting God who never grows tired or weary. (v. 28) After all, the Lord can strengthen the weak and increase the weak's power (Isaiah v. 29). But for those who trust and wait on the Lord, they will have renewed strength. (v. 31). The reward of waiting on God and trusting him comes with the ability to soar through adversity, run through life's challenges, and walk-in victory every day.

Timeout Takeaways

God is greater than our circumstances.

Sometimes, life feels like a long, hard race. At times, the journey seems easy. You have everything you want -- the job you want, or you have the spouse you want, or you have the life you want -- and everything is going smoothly. But then there are times when you don't have the job you want, your spouse is talking about leaving you, or you wake up one day wondering how life got to be such a mess. Your life goes from smooth sailing to a downward spiral. During hard times, it's important to remember that God is greater than our circumstances. There is nothing too big or too hard for God.

God is greater than our doubts.

With tears streaming down my face, I kept moving toward the finish line. I finished the Firecracker Ride, but not without help. I am grateful for the kind people God sent who spoke words of life to me as I struggled to get to the top of the hill. In addition to words of encouragement, my second wind came when I believed God was greater than my doubts. God is always ready to refresh us and offer us our second wind, but we have to want to receive it.

God is greater than our obstacles.

Toward the ride's end, the last obstacle between me and the finish line was a very steep hill. My legs were tired by this point, and I was ready to give my new clip-in pedals a rest. I wanted to get off my bike and walk to the finish line. But I had to remember that God is greater than any obstacle I had to face in both life and this challenging ride. To distract myself from doubt and negative self-talk, I hearing God say in his word, Fear not, for I am with you (Isaiah 41:10). I also changed the music on my phone to hear Marvin Sapp sing a song called, He Has His Hands On You. Before I knew it, I saw a parking lot filled with cyclists. Then I saw my husband, and I knew I had reached the finish line.

GRATEFUL

What are you grateful for today?

LISTENING

Ask God to show you how to deal with obstacles as they come into your life.

OBSERVATION

Read Isaiah 40.

WITNESS

Talk to someone about the time when God helped to overcome a difficult obstacle in your life.

DAY 20 - TIME TO GO DEEPER

Note to self:

Thank you for waking me up to the truth about my identity as a believer.

For too long, my vision was blurred. I used to think that once I gave you my life, that was it until I met you in heaven. But I realized now that was selfish. Forgive me for all the times I thought it was someone else's job to tell others about you, Lord.

No more. I've wasted too much time. Your business is my business. I want to see life from your perspective, Jesus. Thank you for the young lady you sent to me yesterday, confused and looking for answers. I told her all about you. Please open my eyes to see my next assignment from heaven.

I'm available to you.

DAY 20 - TIME TO GO DEEPER

[4] **When He had finished speaking, He said to Simon, "Put out into deep water and let down your nets for a catch."**

[5] **"Master," Simon replied, "we've worked hard all night long and caught nothing! But at Your word, I'll let down the nets."**

[6] **When they did this, they caught a great number of fish, and their nets began to tear.**

[7] **So they signaled to their partners in the other boat to come and help them; they came and filled both boats so full that they began to sink.**

Luke 5:4-7

My grandparents loved to fish. I could listen to their fishing stories for hours. They talked about the best lakes to go to, the best fishing rods to use, and the best bait. They sounded more like professionals than amateurs. When I was 11, I heard my grandmother ask my mother if they could take my brother and me on their next fishing trip. I was so excited I could hardly contain myself. I was finally going on my first fishing trip.

My grandmother fried chicken and packed a cooler with drinks and snacks for the big day. Next, my grandmother and my mother, and I went to the backyard to dig for worms. After wetting the ground, my mother used the shovel to dig up the soil. Since she thought the worms were gross, I grabbed all the worms I could. My grandmother mostly supervised and laughed at my mom and me. After storing our bait, we went to bed.

With the car fully packed, we headed out at 3 a.m. to be on the lake by 4. My grandfather set up my fishing pole and told me to watch closely for any sign of movement. After about an hour of no action, I was frustrated and sleepy. Fishing wasn't anything like I thought it would be. Tired and hungry for the fried chicken, I was relieved of my duties and told I could get back in the car to eat and go back to sleep. By the time I woke up, it was time to go home. As we drove away, I took one last look at the lake and thought, 'I didn't even catch one fish.'

In Luke 5, we find Jesus giving Peter fishing instructions. Jesus said, "Now go out where it is deeper and let down your nets and you will catch a lot of fish!" (v. 4) Peter, who had a fishing business with James and John, believed he knew how to fish. He quickly explained to Jesus what had already been done in trying to catch fish. Fishing on the Sea of Galilee meant standing on the shore or going out in a boat at night. After a while, the fishers pulled the nets out of the water by hand. However, on this night, the men couldn't seem to catch any fish.

But Peter gave into Jesus's recommendation and tried again. (v. 5) With the nets now in deeper water, something unexpected happened. The nets were full. When the men tried to pull the nets up from the water, the nets started to tear from the fish's weight. (v. 6) The men in the boat shouted for help. By now, there were two boats full of fish on the verge of sinking (v. 7).

After seeing the amount of fish, Peter felt ashamed. Realizing that Jesus indeed was the Holy Son of God, he fell to his knees and begged Jesus to leave him because he was a sinful man (v. 8). But Jesus tells Peter not to be afraid. Instead, he invites Peter to fish for people. (v. 10)

The same invitation is open to every believer as part of the Great Commission where Jesus said, "God authorized and commanded me to commission you: Go out and train everyone you meet, far and near, in this way of life, marking them by baptism in the threefold name: Father, Son, and Holy Spirit." (Matthew 28:18) Because of our relationship with Christ, we have a tremendous responsibility to serve as disciple-makers.

Timeout Takeaways

Go into the deep.

As an experienced fisherman, Peter believed fishing near land at night was the only way to catch fish. But Jesus told him to go into deep water during the day to catch fish. Although he hesitated, Peter followed Jesus's instructions and witnessed the tremendous amount of fish caught in the nets. Peter's fishing story proves what can happen when we listen to the voice of God. Despite our knowledge and training, we can't know everything. As disciples of Christ, it should be comforting to know we can always go to God for direction, especially as we share God's word with others. To find people in need of God's love and salvation, we may have to go to unexpected places to reach people in unexpected ways.

Let down the nets.

After putting the nets in the water, the catch of fish was enormous. So big that the boats started to sink. The amount of fish the men were able to pull in would be a blessing to many people. Once Peter realized he was in the presence of holiness, he was ashamed. He fell before Jesus, saying, "Go away from me, because I'm a sinful man, Lord" (v. 8). In addition to being blessed with a huge catch, Peter saw the blessing in recognizing his sin. As we build our relationship with Christ, we can begin to recognize our sin.

Fish for people.

Feeling afraid and ashamed, Peter begs Jesus to leave him. But he doesn't. Instead, Jesus tells Peter, "Don't be afraid. From now on, your work will be to bring people, not fish." (v. 10) True discipleship is committed to the mission of Jesus to make disciples. By the time Jesus reached the end of his earthly ministry, he had instructed his disciples to go out into the world to spread the gospel and make disciples in all the nations. (Matthew 28:19-20) Present-day disciples cannot respond to the person of Christ without responding to the mission of Christ. We all have a responsibility to go deep, let down our nets, and fish for people.

GRATEFUL

What are you grateful for today?

LISTENING

Ask God to show you how to make disciples of Christ.

OBSERVATION

Read Luke 5.

WITNESS

Tell someone about how you met Jesus Christ.

DAY 21 - TIME TO WALK IN VICTORY

Note to self:

Dear Lord,

Thank you for giving me the strength to stand today. Because of you, I walk in victory every day. Because of you, I have been changed from the inside out. Thanks to you, I have a new heart and a renewed mind. I'm sorry for resisting you for so long. Wherever you take me, let others see you in me. When people ask me for a reason for my faith, let me always have an answer. Lead me to the people who need to hear a word of encouragement, and I will gladly tell them about you, Jesus.

My soul will boast in you, Lord.

DAY 21 - TIME TO WALK IN VICTORY

Jesus said, "Get up, take your bedroll, start walking."

John 5:8

Cliff Shiepe needed a miracle. While in his mid-twenties, Cliff was suddenly hit by an illness that caused dizziness, nausea, fatigue, high fevers, and water retention. Instead of moving forward with his life, Cliff was bed-ridden, unable to work or live alone. After seven years and 70 doctors, Cliff met a doctor who prescribed a straightforward remedy:

a ten-day fast of no food, only water. Initially, Cliff thought the idea of no food for ten was terrifying, but he was desperate. He gave it a try and the fast worked. The fevers, inflammation, and water retention were gone. Cliff's energy returned, and he started working out every day. Cliff thanked God for his miracle.

In John 5, Jesus meets a man who needed a miracle. The pool of Bethesda had five covered porches surrounded by sick people, including a man who suffered from a paralytic condition. In addition to the man, the people lying by the pool were blind, disabled, lame, and paralyzed (v. 3). Despite their different conditions, everyone waiting by the pool wanted one thing to happen: an angel to stir the water. Many believed the first person to step into the water after the angel stirred the water would be healed.

The man lying by the pool had been sick for 38 years. When Jesus saw the man, he asked him, "Do you want to be well?" Instead of giving Jesus a yes or no answer immediately, the man told Jesus that he didn't have the help he needed to get into the pool (v. 7). He said every time he tried to get into the water, someone else stepped in front of him. After listening to the man's response, Jesus told him, "Stand up! Pick up your mat and walk." (v. 8) Without hesitation, the man picked up his mat and started walking. He was healed.

Of the people lying around the pool, waiting for the water to be stirred, Jesus could have picked anyone. Jesus could have healed every one. Instead, he focused on building one man's faith and making him an example for all to see. When Jesus told the man to stand up, he did not hesitate. The man stood immediately, rolled up his bed, and started to walk. Later, when Jesus found the man in the Temple, he said, "You are well now. But stop sinning, or something worse may happen to you." (v.14)

The Bible warns us that the wages of sin are death (Romans 6:23). Once we repent and God brings us out of the difficult places in our life, he doesn't want us to go back to the way we were. Anytime Jesus brings us out, he wants us to follow the path of righteousness. Because of our relationship with Jesus, we can walk in victory every day.

Timeout Takeaways

Trust Jesus to know everything.

When going through life's challenges, do you ever feel like no one understands what you're going through? Not even God? But the word tells us that even the very hairs of your head are all numbered (Luke 12:7). Therefore, Jesus knows everything about us. He knows about all of your hurts, pains, and disappointments. During tough times, I find comfort in knowing that Jesus is the Victorious One (Revelation 3:21). When we allow the Victorious One to get us back on our feet, we can walk in victory.

Trust Jesus to do the unexpected.

Have you ever received a gift you weren't expecting? It's often a pleasant surprise. Imagine how the paralyzed man waiting for healing must have felt. He thought his healing would come by getting into the pool after an angel stirred the water. Little did he know that's not how he would receive his blessing. Instead, Jesus showed up and did the unexpected by healing the man instantly. Sometimes we put limits on Jesus by thinking there's only one way he can deliver us from crippling situations. But when we pray and invite Jesus to take over, we can trust him to not only deliver us but to do the unexpected.

Trust Jesus to help you move forward.

Once Cliff regained his strength, he was ready to get out and start moving. One of the first things he did was hire a trainer to work with him at a local gym. Soon, he published a novel, *Cliff Falls*, a Christian suspense novel that offers hope. Today, Cliff

122

travels the world talking about his book and sharing his testimony. When Jesus healed the man at the pool of Bethesda, he immediately got up and started moving. Not only does Jesus want to heal us, but he wants to see us move on from our crippling experiences. And we can't forget that others are watching us. As we trust Jesus, our example may help others know what they should do when experiencing challenges in life. Your victory walk will not be in vain if you can lead someone into the loving arms of Jesus.

GRATEFUL

What are you grateful for today?

LISTENING

Ask God to reveal any part of our spiritual walk that is lame or not moving.

OBSERVATION

Read John 5.

WITNESS

Talk to someone about a time when you were down, and God lifted you.

I feel like everything was going great in my career before I got laid off. Now I don't know what to do next.

Being let go from a job is never easy. If you're like me, you probably had your career mapped out until retirement. Once I graduated from college, I envisioned going from being a public relations assistant account executive to vice president in one straight shot. According to my plan, I worked as long as I wanted at every company that hired me. I saw myself gliding from one position to the next without any setbacks or disappointments. But life doesn't always go according to the plans we write down. I know this all too well now.

After lots of tears, frustration, and talks with God, it all clicked. It was time to surrender to God's plan for my life. Right here. Right now. I decided to focus on Proverbs 3:5-6:

> *Trust God from the bottom of your heart; don't try to figure out everything on your own.*

> *Listen for God's voice in everything you do, everywhere you go; he's the one who will keep you on track.*

Knowing complete surrender to God would be a challenge for me, I decided to meditate on Proverbs 3 for weeks. I wanted to:

124

- Let go of any doubts or fears about being laid off.
- Take God at his word and stand on His promises.
- Listen to the voice of God in moving forward with my career.
- Embrace the next chapter of my life.

I wanted to trust God's plan for my life with all my heart. To do so, I knew that meant spending time with God to get clarity on His plan for my life. So this meant:

- Reading, studying, and writing God's word (I learn better when I write things down)
- Praying and asking God to open my eyes and ears to new opportunities
- Reading articles and taking free online classes.
- Exploring my feelings and new ideas by writing in my journal
- Envisioning myself living the life God intended for me

Do you find yourself feeling like you are off course? Here are a few things you can do:

Lay your heartaches at the feet of Jesus. Use prayer and journal writing as a way to let God know how you feel. What hurts? What are your concerns? Be honest about how you feel.

Be prepared to let go. Make time in your schedule to read God's word and pray. Ask God to reveal His truth to you. Don't hold on to the pain that comes with disappointment. Open your heart to feel God's love and grace in your situation.

Open your eyes to new possibilities. As you spend time with God, look for new opportunities. Don't limit God, and don't limit yourself. Be open to new things and adventures.

Ask God for a new direction. Before you begin the next chapter of your life, ask God what He wants to see you do and where He would like you to go. God has a plan for your life. Ask Him where He wants you to go next.

Thank you for joining me on this 21-day journey. I thank God for opening my eyes to new topics he wants me to study and share with others. Over time, I have embraced the call to grow in the grace and knowledge of our Lord and Savior, Jesus Christ. (2 Peter 3:18)

Since leaving corporate life in 2017, God has blessed me to build a new life. I am happy to report that my business, Constant Communicators, is doing well to help clients with their writing and public relations projects. I thank God for ordering my steps. I am grateful for the new doors God opens and for the doors he keeps shut.

After writing my first book, *Time to Refresh*, God told me to keep writing. Writing *Time to Reset* allowed me the opportunity to examine myself and focus on areas where I could improve my walk with Christ. The experience was eye-opening, revealing more than 21 opportunities for spiritual growth. As I started to write my second book, I used God's word to remind myself of the following statements :

- I will trust the Lord completely, and I won't depend on my knowledge. (Proverbs 3:5)

- If God is for me, no one can stand against me. And God is with me. He even let his own Son suffer for me. God gave his Son for all of us. So now, with Jesus, God will surely give me all things. (Romans 8:31-32)

- So, Lord, I will tell people how good you are. I will praise you all day long. (Psalm 35:28)

If you ask me how I'm doing any day of the week, I'll tell you I am grateful.

My continual prayer is that the words of my mouth, and the meditation of my heart, be acceptable in thy sight, O LORD, because you are my strength and my redeemer.

Walking in Victory!

ACKNOWLEDGMENTS

This book would not be possible without the help of many wonderful, loving people. I'm grateful for all the support I've received from family, friends, and mentors. I am grateful to God for blessing me continuously and for answering my prayers. I'm grateful for my husband, Kelvin, for demonstrating true love since the day we met and for being my best friend for life. I'm grateful for my son, Cole, for being the best son a mother could ever imagine.

I'm grateful for my mother, Edna Brown, and my aunt, Jeffie Jackson, for giving me everything I ever needed, including all the love and support I could ever ask for. I'm grateful for my brother, James Brown, for always encouraging me and promoting my latest projects.

I'm grateful for my entire family in Savannah, Georgia, especially my cousin Cheryl Barnes for supporting my first book and always speaking words of love and support. I'm grateful to my niece, Payton, who always makes me laugh, and for her mom, Robinette, for extending kindness during the launch of my first book. I'm grateful to my brother and sister-in-love, Karsten and Pam, for more than 25 years of love, and to my late mother-in-love, Beverly Tyson, for accepting me as her bonus daughter.

I'm grateful for my spiritual parents, Pastor T.L. and Elder Rebecca Carmichael for always encouraging me and opening my eyes to the truth of God's word.

I'm grateful to Amy Lou Anderson and Traci Higgins for your encouraging words of love and your help in selecting the book's cover design. I'm grateful for Denise Campana for always being calm and wise and for your support in helping find new book cover designs.

I'm forever grateful to Lucy Levett for being a true sister in Christ who always makes time for me, including participating in the selection process for the book's cover design. I'm grateful for Robin Byrd for always making time to talk about my dreams and plans.

I'm grateful for all of the beautiful women of Elevation Baptist Church who showed me so much love by purchasing my first book. Finally, I'm grateful to the many people I haven't explicitly mentioned who pray for and encourage me, thank you.

Karen Brown Tyson is an award-winning author. Her first book, ***Time to Refresh: A 21-Day Devotional to Renew Your Mind After Being Laid Off, Fired or Sidelined***, was named 2019 Finalist in the Religion: Christian Inspirational Category of the 2019 Best Book Awards.

Karen has a Bachelor of Arts degree in English from West Virginia University and a Master of Arts in English from National University. In addition, she has a Master of Arts degree in Christian Ministry and postgraduate certificates in Christian Leadership, Theological Studies and Biblical Studies from Liberty University Rawlings School of Divinity. Her ministry concentration focuses on the expository teaching of the Word of God in the areas of spiritual discipline, discipleship, leadership, apologetics and New Testament theology.

Karen has served in God's kingdom in a variety of ways including her most recent assignments with the Deacon's Wives, Women, Evangelism, Social Media and Helps ministries at her church, Elevation Baptist Church. Karen also serves as the Dean of the Elevation Bible Institute where she teaches courses on spiritual discipline, evangelism, and Christian apologetics.

Karen is a graduate of the Jerry Jenkins Christian Writer's Guild apprentice program. As a writer, she has developed several Christian ministry tools and training materials for her local church.

Karen and her husband of 25 years, Kelvin, have one son and they live in North Carolina.

Day 5

Elison, Logan. "A Divine Rescue from the Depths" https://www.guideposts.org/faith-and-prayer/prayer-stories/answered-prayers/a-divine-rescue-from-the-depths. 29 July, 2014.

Day 17

Blackaby, Henry; Avery Willis. *On Mission with God: Living God's Purpose for His Glory.* Nashville: Boardman & Holman Publishers, 2002, 143.

Evans, Tony, and CSB B. Holman. *The Tony Evans Bible Commentary: Advancing God's Kingdom Agenda.* , 2019. Kindle version.

Day 18

Evans, Tony, and CSB B. Holman. Ezekiel: Prophecies of Israel's Restoration (33:1 – 39:29) *The Tony Evans Bible Commentary: Advancing God's Kingdom Agenda.* , 2019. Kindle version

Day 19

Guzik, David. "Study Guide for Isaiah." Enduring Word Bible Commentary.

Day 21

Shiepe, Cliff. "How to Make the Most of a Miracle" https://www.guideposts.org/better-living/health-and-wellness/coping-with-illness/how-to-make-the-most-of-a-miracle. 25 September, 2020.

INSPIRATION

What inspires you? Did you read anything that motivates you? Take note.

2

THANKS FOR READING, TIME TO RESET!

If you enjoyed this book, please consider sharing the message with others.

- Mention the book in a Twitter update, Facebook post, Pinterest pin, blog post, or upload a picture to Instagram.

- Recommend the book to people in your small group study, book club, workplace and classes.

- Pick up a copy for someone you know who would be inspired by the book.

- Share a book review on Amazon .

Visit my website at www.karenbrowntyson.com to learn more about my Time to Grow in Grace series and my next book, **Time to Rejoice: A 21-Day Devotional to Renew Your Mind After Being Knocked Off Course, Let Down or Broken.** Scheduled for release in 2021.

Made in the USA
Las Vegas, NV
13 February 2021

17816421R00075